GEORGE
MATHIS

PINO GRANDE

Logging Railroads of the Michigan-California Lumber Co.

PINO GRANDE

Logging Railroads of the
Michigan-California Lumber Company

BY R. S. POLKINGHORN

BERKELEY, CALIFORNIA · 1966

HOWELL
-NORTH
BOOKS

PINO GRANDE — Logging Railroads of the Michigan-California Lumber Co.

Printed and bound in the United States of America

Library of Congress Catalog Card No. 66-30010

||||||||||||||||||||||||||||||||||||||||||||||||||

ENDPAPERS
Pencil sketch by George Mathis.

FRONTISPIECE
The beautifully detailed little Shay had received excellent care and provided a proud and attractive background, on the Slab Creek bridge below Pino Grande, for this group portrait with the president of the lumber company and his wife. *(Both photographs: R. L. Smirle Collection.)*

||||||||||||||||||||||||||||||||||||||||||||||||||

Published by
HOWELL-NORTH BOOKS
1050 Parker Street, Berkeley, California 94710

Preface

When a Coloradan moves to California, he is likely to bring with him a deep affection for narrow gauge railroads. If so, he will surely feel at home in the Sierras which abound with their remains. He will also discover that it is a very short step indeed from narrow gauge mining roads to narrow gauge logging roads. A Shay is after all a steam engine and every bit as fascinating as the South Park Consolidations that used to thread their way along the South Platte River, and by my home, south of Denver.

It matters not where one lives in California. The fossils of a dozen or more small logging lines clamor for the newcomer's attention. Sacramento is no exception. Towle Brothers, Birce & Smart Lumber Co., Reed Timber & Lumber Co., Diamond & Caldor Railroad are all within fifty miles and each has its charms for the railroad fan; but the Michigan-California Lumber Co. with its justly famous cable is a very special case. The cable itself was only recently gone when as a newcomer, I got my first look at the only remaining major artifact — the North Cable Tower! High above the river on Cable Point, it immediately excited what is likely to be a lifelong interest.

It was therefore no surprise to discover that Michigan-California Lumber Co. and its predecessors had commanded the interest, concern, and affection of a host of people during its sixty years of railroad logging. Its comings and goings were lavishly chronicled in the local papers; its incidents and accidents were recorded in the memories of employees. Most important of all it attracted one photographer after another even in its earliest days. Several of them had great skill and many hundreds of pictures were treasured and saved.

Special note should be made of the collection of photographs taken in the early 1900s by Turrill & Miller Photographers of San Francisco. Most of them are preserved in the family album of R. L. Smirle, son of an officer of El Dorado Lumber Co. and were made available for this book by Mr. Smirle.

There are many other persons to whom the author is indebted for pictures or bits of information. The debt to Pete Boromini is especially large. He joined the company in 1914, became a locomotive engineer within a few years and remained in the cab until the last narrow gauge firebox grew cold. His memories of events, people and locomotives have proved accurate and voluminous. Without his help many many photographs would have gone unidentified or mislabeled.

Michigan-California Lumber Co. through its president, Mr. John Blodgett, Jr., and especially through its office manager, George Burrows, gave much help to this history. Mr. Burrows spent many hours looking through company records for items of interest. Long, productive and very interesting interviews were granted to the author by many other former and current employees including Tom Jinkerson, Jack Williams, Curtis Perrce, Tom Berthelot, Rudy Previc, Mrs. Edgar Kimble whose husband was a long-time C.P.&L.T. engineer and Mrs. Jack Corker. Mrs. Corker's late husband, an officer of the firm, had an excellent collection of photographs from which she has kindly provided a large number.

Mr. Swift Berry who managed the firm from the late 1920s to the early 1950s took time to read the manuscript with great care. So did his son, Jack Berry, and through their efforts many of the technical errors of an author without experience in the logging industry were eliminated.

I owe a special debt to Sam Taylor who drew all of the maps as a labor of love.

When I remember these people and the many others with whom I reminisced about railroad logging on the Georgetown Divide, I count the hours spent on this book as among the most pleasant I have known.

R. S. POLKINGHORN

Sacramento, California
1966

There was plenty of slab wood to fuel the engines in the woods. Here is a 1941 view of Shay No. 6 wooding up near Pino Grande. *(Russ Ahrnke Photo.)*

Table of Contents

In this quarry, shown as it appeared before 1895, prisoners at Folsom Prison cut most of the stone that went into the dam at Folsom and the canal. The railroad spur which serviced this quarry connected with the line from Folsom to the dam site during construction. At Folsom the track connected with the Sacramento Valley Railroad, California's first railway. *(California Division of Beaches & Parks)*

CHAPTER I

Dry Run 1888-1889

It was the steam logging railroad that made it possible to harvest the sugar pine forests on the slopes of the Sierras in California. Early attempts to use flumes or river drives gave way in the early 1900s to the economics of railroading. By 1930 the mountains had been conquered by a myriad of small, independent logging lines. Not the least of these was the narrow gauge Michigan-California Lumber Co. railroad. Its tracks wound like silver threads around the hills and up the valleys of the Georgetown Divide, a ridge that runs westward from Lake Tahoe to the Central Valley of California. On the slopes of the ridge, grew what lumbermen were referring to in the late 1800s as "the finest growth of sugar pine of any section of the state; trees growing up to eight and ten feet in diameter being quite common." This book is concerned with the history of the Michigan-California Lumber Co. up to the end of its railroad logging days in 1951.

The company did not at first intend to use a railroad. Nor had it conceived the cableway across the South Fork of the American River for which it was to become so famous. The early view of railroad logging was not promising. The lumberman's journal, *Pacific Coast Wood and Iron,* commented in December 1889, "The timber of the Georgetown Divide has been inaccessible, owing to the roughness of the country and its very considerable elevation above the line of the Central Pacific Railroad. Railroads would to a limited extent [open up the timber] but building railway lines along all the canyons could not be expected."[24]* The first attempt to log on the Divide called for floating the logs down the South Fork of the American River to a mill in the foothills. River drives were very successful in the Appalachians, in Wisconsin and Michigan, and even in Oregon and Washington. However, experiments with river driving in

the Sierras were generally failures, because of shortage of water in the rocky narrow canyons.

This history begins in 1866 when Horatio Gates Livermore, an early immigrant from New England, bought a small tract of timber on the South Fork of the American River and began to build a dam near the town of Folsom, where the river leaves the foothills for the broad Central Valley. The dam was to provide a still water basin for the logs he expected to drive about forty miles down the river and it would also provide water power for industry in the manner of many small New England mill towns with which Livermore was familiar. He had driven a few logs down the river the preceding year and found it very difficult without the help of a still water basin to take them out of the swift current at Folsom. At first he expected others would drive logs to the sawmills in Folsom, too. He asked the Placer County supervisors for a franchise to "construct a boom [to collect the logs] and maintain it for twenty years . . . to collect and receive the sum of $1.50 per 1000 board feet of logs, timber and lumber as may be rafted or floated to said boom." This, too, was a common Eastern practice at the time.

Work on the dam was slow and expensive; over $100,000 was spent on footings and a railroad spur to connect the dam site with the Sacramento Valley Railroad at Folsom. So great was the expense, in fact, that work was soon abandoned. In 1868 Livermore tried to arrange an exchange with the State of California that would provide prison labor to work on the dam. He offered a large piece of land near Folsom as a prison site in exchange for the labor. Though the deal was nominally completed in 1868, it was not until 1888 that agreement between Livermore and the State was reached over the amount of the labor involved, and convicts began in earnest to build the dam.

Once work began, the convicts put in 520,000 man-days in six years between 1888 and 1893. The prison often found itself short of labor and in 1889

---

*Superior figures in text refer to numbered entries in the list of Sources, following the Appendix.

In February of 1890, the Folsom *Telegraph* announced: "We have seen one of the four immense log wagons the [American River Land & Lumber] company is building. They are as strong as good wood and iron can make them. The wheels are made of solid blocks of sugar pine 14 inches thick at the hub and 7 inches at the tire. Only the best Norway iron has been used. Each wagon is capable of sustaining a load of 20 tons. . . . They will be pulled by eight yoke of oxen each." *(Perry Baker Collection)*

Logging in El Dorado County

Warden Aull noted in his monthly report that "unless we receive more consideration from the superior courts than we have in the last three months, we will close the year with but a few more than 300 prisoners." It seems likely that he wanted more prisoners assigned to his prison and not more convictions, but he did not say so.

Prison labor was valued at 50 cents per day per man but was actually worth much more to the company. Convicts built a dam 89 feet high and 450 feet long across the top that backed up water for four miles. They built a granite canal 50 feet wide and eight feet deep to carry logs to the mill pond and water to an electric generating plant. The notion that Folsom would become a "New England mill town" with many small water-powered industries had been dropped and an electric generating plant was begun instead. Power generated at this plant was soon being transmitted 21½ miles to Sacramento for street railways, in what came to be considered an important early experiment in long-distance power transmission. The power plant operated from 1895 until 1952 when it was included as part of a state park.

In March, 1889, soon after the dam was well under way, Livermore formed the American River Land & Lumber Co. and revived his plans for logging on the Georgetown Divide. The company made its first purchase of timberlands from the Central Pacific Railroad. Logging actually began when Colonel George W. Cummins, an Eastern lumberman and first superintendent of the company, took a crew of twenty men, several teams, and a complete outfit to the woods on June 15, 1890. The first logs were cut at Iowa Canyon, on the south side of the American River, but operations soon shifted to Slab Creek, on the north or Georgetown Divide side of the river.

Logs were cut in the winter from October to February when the sap is down because it was thought at the time that a sugar pine log full of sap would not float. Actually butt logs and sometimes second cuts are always "sinkers" because of the greater density of the wood near the base of the tree trunk. The logs were hauled to the river by team and the newspaper reported in the summer of 1891 that "cattle are being shod preparatory to starting the immense log trucks [large wheeled wagons] built during the past winter." How the first logs were put in the river is unknown, but as soon as operations shifted to the north side, a chute was constructed down Slab Creek from a point near the present settlement of Mosquito, where in those days there was a small mill.

According to Ed Morton, who worked on the first log drives, there was a little log yard on a flat a quarter mile below that mill. A couple of hundred feet below this was the beginning of the log chute, to which logs were dragged in strings of about five, by an upright steam donkey. The two-poled chute had log poles about thirty inches in diameter, set several inches apart to form a trough, and held in place by small blocking logs on either side. The chute ran down the bottom of a ravine and through a deep cut into the river. When heavy timber could not be transported, because of insufficient water, ties were cut and moved through a V-shaped tie flume with 16-inch sides just west of the chute. About 35 men kept this woods operation going.

Boats were used during the log drives to carry the men along with the logs and to take them back and forth across the river as they broke the dams and kept the logs moving. Maneuvering these boats was a dangerous business, requiring great skill. In Ed Morton's words:

> When the first boat started on the first log drive, I was in it at one oar, an Indian boy at another and a Swede at the back of the boat with a pike pole. The Swede got his pole caught between some rocks when the boat was right opposite the mouth of the log chute. The crazy Swede couldn't get the pole loose and wouldn't let go. I was pulling for all I was worth on the oar. The Indian told me to be careful, that we'd be sunk if I broke an oar. I said, "Well, let me hit that crazy Swede over the head with it, then." About that time the current pulled the pole out of the Swede's hands and the boat went on down and we beached it. Just then a string of logs roared down the chute into the river.

> They lost a lot of boats in that rocky river bed. Usually they took them down the narrow places with snub ropes handled by men on the shore. But one Indian from Canada was really handy with a boat. He got to drinking and took the boat down the rapids by the swinging bridge [at the site of the present Old Mosquito Road bridge] at flood stage without hitting a rock. All the time he was singing and shrieking at the top of his voice.

Logs were turned into the river in the spring of 1891 and first reached the dam at Folsom on May 14. As the logs passed through the town of Salmon Falls, five miles above the dam, townspeople turned out to watch. This small town was the site of the most difficult part of the river. Here, in ad-

The Chute Camp, at the left, was opened by the American River Land & Lumber Co. in 1891 as base for construction and operations of the log chute. Ten years later it served similarly during construction of the cable by the El Dorado Lumber Co. Yarding of logs from the stump to the head of the chute was accomplished by horses or bulls before the Dolbeer steam donkey came into use in the early 1900s. The chute dumped the logs into the American River where experienced river drivers took over the job of floating them to the mill at Folsom. *(Above: Michigan-California Lumber Co. Collection; below: Perry Baker Collection)*

dition to the falls, the logs had to be helped over a water-diversion dam owned by the Natomas Water & Mining Co., another Livermore firm. These two hazards could not be overcome when the river was low and by June of 1891 "rapidly falling water had made the drive less successful than was anticipated." In fact, only about 700,000 board feet* reached the dam, although 2,000,000 feet were started. The rest were stranded at Salmon Falls. In an effort to salvage something from the 1890-91 season, a portion of the remaining logs were cut into 20,000 railroad ties and several hundred cords of firewood and sent down the river in that way.

Failure of the first drive started some brief talk about a change in the plans of the American River Land & Lumber Co. A railroad that would run from the timber to some point below the rocky, narrow parts of the gorge was considered. In fact, a survey was made,[12] but no such railroad was built. Flumes were often used in the Sierras and several had been built that were fifty or more miles long, but the suggestion of a flume was also rejected. A number of improvements were made, nevertheless, in an effort to make a better showing the next season. Large boulders were blasted out of the narrow or tightly curved portions of the gorge. To aid the teams and wagons in getting logs to the head of the chute at the river gorge, 12 miles of rail together with spikes and fishplates were bought for a 3-foot gauge logging railroad.

It is said that rail was purchased secondhand in San Francisco where it had been used on cable car tracks. As a matter of fact, early pictures of the tracks show rail of the type often used in city streets with a projection on the side to provide a flangeway in pavement. As late as 1964 several pieces of this type of rail were still lying on ties on a long-abandoned spur.

Charlie Wood, who came to work on the railroad in the early 1890s and stayed on to become logging superintendent for El Dorado Lumber Co. some 10 years later, had another recollection of the first railroad iron: It was "charcoal iron. It caused all kinds of trouble. We had to replace it all. It was high grade iron but no good for railroads." According to Wood it came around the Horn for use on the line from Sacramento to Folsom, the first railroad in California. If he is right, it probably didn't work very well on that railroad

either. Perhaps the lumber company felt when they bought the rail that their rolling stock was light enough for it.

One curious fact about this early railroad construction is that no trestles were built across the many little canyons along the right-of-way. A train of two or three log cars would switch in and out of short tail tracks all the way to the head of the chute. The exact number of these switchbacks is not known, but all were replaced by trestles when the El Dorado Lumber Co. took over in 1900. With the first few miles of track completed by Chinese labor, the loaded log cars could be dropped down to the head of the chute by gravity and the empties were pulled back by horses.

At the foot of the chute was a log basin, formed by a "splash dam" which could furnish a sudden surge of water to "splash" the logs over tight spots in the gorge.

In the late summer of 1891 Colonel Cummins announced enthusiastically, "I am up to my ears in business; in fact I am buried. . . . The railroad will reach our first good timber in a distance of six miles [near the camp which came to be called Old Pino]. There is timber enough to keep us logging for three or four years. . . . This is good news and victory already perches on our Sugar Pine Banners."[26] To this paean the editor of the Georgetown *Gazette* added: "Those who said it couldn't be done are grossly intoxicated by their own verbosity." Whatever the business that buried Colonel Cummins, it could not have been very profitable, since the firm probably had yet to sell its first board. As for the editor, he was destined presently to choke on *his* own verbosity.

The 1891-92 season started well. Warm rains in April raised the river enough to start the logs. The Placerville *Mountain Democrat* reported, "We get word that the river at Chili Bar [about a quarter of the way to Folsom] is full of them. The weather, however, has turned a little cooler and the rain ceasing may check the rise of the water for a time, but the snow is in the mountains and must come out." Two weeks later the paper was less optimistic because "a heavy fall of snow occurred in the mountains during the last few days. This checks the flow of water in the American River to some extent, but a few warm days will start it up lively. We learn that logs have been passing Coloma at a lively rate for the past few days." Coloma is located several miles above the special hazards of Salmon Falls. The spring weather remained cool, the snow melted slowly, the river never rose and the logs were stopped at Salmon Falls.

---

*Logs and lumber are measured in board feet. A board foot is enough wood to make a board one foot wide, one foot long and one inch thick.

Colonel Cummins, however, remained "up to his eyes in business." He kept 250 men working on the railroad from the chute back into the timber and used the small sawmill to cut ties and bridge timbers. He rode through Georgetown with wagons on which was loaded a small Porter locomotive, the first engine to be used on the Georgetown Divide. This engine is discussed in the Appendix as locomotive No. 6. "It was a big sight and not a few of our people appeared to behold a railroad locomotive entering town with its bell ringing," said the local paper. Another 25-ton engine (probably Heisler No. 1) was reported on the way.

The summer of 1892 also saw the completion of the first boom. This was a floating barricade of timbers chained to three granite piers set diagonally across the river about one-half mile above the dam in the slack water. The piers were 30 to 40 feet long and 20 to 30 feet wide at the base, and the middle one was more than 60 feet high. The boom itself was made in 11 sections of 12-inch square timbers bolted together into four-foot square sections 50 feet long. These sections were chained together and floated about forty feet downstream from the piers. In the words of the Sacramento *Union*, it constituted "a framework sufficient to support any strain that may be brought to bear upon it." This method of construction was common at the time in the East, and very familiar to Colonel Cummins. However, less than six months later, in December 1892, the boom broke "in the midst of a great gale and freshet" and about half of the logs behind it were lost over the top of the dam. A few days later the newspaper stated, "Colonel Cummins has been superseded as Superintendent of American River Land & Lumber Co."

Logs were delivered into the American River by the long chute which descended about 3000 feet from the edge of the gorge, high above. When completed in 1893, it was reputed to be the longest such structure ever built. Below, Heisler No. 1 still bore the No. 2 plate on its boiler front when this picture was taken, for the No. 1 plate was then on the little 0-4-0T Porter that had been delivered in 1892. The setting of this picture is probably Pino Grande while it was just a logging camp and the mill may be either the one located on this site by Charlie Wood before 1900 or a small company mill used to make ties and bridge timbers. If this is a later picture, the mill may have been the one first used by El Dorado Lumber Co. in 1901. *(Above: Perry Baker Collection; opposite: Michigan-California Lumber Co. Collection)*

Logs for the world's first all-electric sawmill at Folsom, shown in the 1896 picture, above, were driven some 40 miles down the American River and collected in the still water basin formed by the dam. The canal through which logs were floated to the millpond appears, empty of water, in the lower right-hand corner of the picture below. The dam and canal were essentially unchanged in 1941 when the picture was taken, though more than fifty years old.

The mill was never a success. Sketchy newspaper stories indicate that it was not in operation for more than three months during the ten-year history of the American River Land & Lumber Co. In 1901 the saw was moved to Pino Grande, where it was powered by a conventional steam engine of that time. *(Above: John H. Plimpton Collection; below: J. E. Fluharty Photo)*

The break in the boom prevented any drive during the winter of 1892-93, but investment continued and a $15 per share assessment was levied on the stockholders. During the summer of 1893, the railroad reached Camp 4 (Old Pino) about four miles from the chute, and the Porter locomotive was put in operation. A permanent chute 2900 feet long was built down to the river on a 30 degree incline. The head of the chute was on the hill above the mouth of Slab Creek where the logging railroad came out of the woods. It required about 1¼ million board feet of 30-inch diameter logs to form its V-shape, and cost $60,000.

One witness described the trip made by logs down the chute, as follows: "An engine [steam donkey] at the head of the chute hauls the logs by means of wire rope from the rollways [beside the railroad track] in groups of five to eight, and as they reach the verge of the hill, their speed is considerably accelerated; and after passing 100 feet or so down the chute, they vanish in a cloud of smoke caused by their friction in the chute, a rumbling, whizzing sound following them for several seconds and the final plunge into the river being distinctly heard a distance of a mile back from the canyon."[25]

The drive of 1893-94 was also a disappointment. Three million feet of logs were put in the river, but they had only reached Salmon Falls by the time the water fell.

It should be noted that all of these drives were dangerous to the men. The river was narrow and rocky and when the water was high enough to float the logs, it was very fast. Sometimes, of course, danger and death had its grimly comic moments. Often the bodies of men drowned in the river were not found for several months. One body turned up after a long hot summer many miles downstream in a nearly inaccessible part of the gorge. Charlie Winchell, the coroner, was called to climb down into the gorge and identify the body. He went down drunk and angry because it was such hard going. By the time he reached the bottom he was so angry that he kicked the shrunken corpse. Then he hired a Russian to pick up the remains and carry them to the top of the hill for five dollars.

The drive of 1894-95 was the most nearly successful ever made. High water in the river made it possible for logs previously stranded at Salmon Falls to be brought the rest of the way to the boom at Folsom. In addition, 4 million board feet of new logs were started from the chute. The last

of the new logs arrived at Salmon Falls in August, 1894, after making the trip at the approximate rate of three miles per day. An attempt to use a new by-pass canal around the falls and the water diversion dam was a failure, and once again the new logs were stopped at that spot.

After the partial success of this drive, the Folsom mill was pushed to completion by December, 1896. It had a nine-foot, electrically driven, single-band saw, with a capacity of 75,000 board feet per day. Lumber journals report it to have been the first electrically driven sawmill in the world; and as such, it was many years ahead of its time.

Before this only small quantities of lumber had been cut in Folsom by a small, temporary mill set up near the boom. The lumber was all used by the company itself. With the main mill now complete logs were allowed to move from the boom into the canal to float down to the mill pond. An immediate dispute broke out with the prison over opening the headgates on the canal far enough to let logs through. The canal ran along one side of the prison grounds and the warden feared that prisoners would dive into the canal and swim under the headgates and out of the prison. It was probably not necessary to settle the dispute for the mill operated only three months cutting up the logs on hand.

Ten million board feet, the annual capacity of the mill, were most likely cut that winter, 1896-97, but the logs did not reach Folsom. The mill "temporarily" closed in March 1897 to await new logs and apparently remained idle through 1898. While it has been reported that two successful log drives were conducted in 1898, this is unlikely in view of the idleness of the mill and in the absence of newspaper reports on them. No reason was given for the failure of the logs to reach the mill in those seasons, but presumably low water was the cause. One newspaper commented wryly, "The mill, at the present time, is not what might be termed a bonanza."

In 1898, just in time for the last operations of American River Land & Lumber Co., the Heisler locomotive arrived and was set up at Pino Grande camp. Pino Grande, called "Pye-no Grand" by the French Canadians, Greeks, and Chinese who logged and built railroads there, was the farthest penetration of the woods in the 1890s. It was just a logging camp at the time but in 1900 it became the site of the main rough-cut sawmill and remained so until the end of railroad logging in 1950.

"High waters," like the one shown in the 1911 picture below, twice broke the lumber boom during the 1890s to let the logs go over the top of the dam and on down the river. Of the boom that once held back the logs and guided them into the canal, only the massive granite piers to which it had been chained remained in 1941. The middle pier, nearly covered with sand and gravel in the picture above, was sixty feet high. (Above: J. E. Fluharty Photo, U. S. Bureau of Reclamation; below: California Division of Beaches & Parks)

American River Dam during High Water 1911.

In this, the last season for American River Land & Lumber Co., twenty million board feet of logs lay on the ground around Pino Grande ready for the trip to Folsom. The people of Folsom waited for the winter rains that would raise the river, bring the logs, open the mill and bring prosperity to the community. They did not wait in vain. In early March the rains came and came. The stranded logs at Salmon Falls floated into the boom. So did the first of the twenty million feet of new logs. The basin filled with logs and the water rose until, at 11:00 a.m. on March 25, 1899, the boom broke again. Logs went over the top of the dam until at least three million feet were lost. They were scattered down the American and Sacramento Rivers all the way for about fifty miles to Rio Vista and an attempt was made to sell these choice sugar pine logs to farmers along the river for firewood. The exact extent of the loss is both unknown and irrelevant. The logs were under attachment to creditors and by December much other property—including the little Porter, first locomotive on the Georgetown Divide—was being sold or pledged. This was the end of the American River Land & Lumber Co. It is said that the company spent nearly a million dollars in those ten years without any year producing a profit. It was not lack of capital or determination that produced the failure, but lack of water. Years later Al Greeley, a man who worked on several early drives recalled, "They sent for the finest river drivers they could find. They went to Canada for most of them, they were fine men, all over six feet and tough. They were hard working, hard drinking men but this river just couldn't be drove. They used tons and tons of powder trying to make a channel. It was just about impossible to move out a key log when there was a jam like they do back home. The logs were just too heavy. I used to write home about the condition of the river and the size of the logs, big six- and seven-foot sticks, and they wouldn't believe me."

From all this investment, the power plant remains as a museum. The log pond and one corner of the mill foundation can be located. The canal is there but the dam was removed in 1952 and replaced by a much larger one. The first nine miles of railroad from the chute to Pino Grande can be followed into the woods as a line of rotted ties and burned trestles that does not even hint at the importance railroad logging would attain during the following half century.

As was noted earlier, this logging and lumber enterprise was begun by Horatio Gates Livermore in 1866, not many years after he left New England to establish the Livermore family in Northern California. This enterprise was only one of many that he promoted in the Folsom area until his death in 1879.[3] Two of his sons, Charles E. and Horatio Putnam Livermore continued the development of logging on the Georgetown Divide until the failure of the American River Land & Lumber Co. in 1899, an event which ended the role of the Livermores in this history. It did not end their interest in the Folsom area and in Northern California generally. They have remained an important family in the region to the present day.

The original cable of the El Dorado Lumber Co. did not change much after this picture was taken, in the early 1900s, for over two decades. In its time it hauled 25 billion board feet of lumber across this gorge. *(Perry Baker Collection)*

CHAPTER II

On the Auction Block Again 1900-1907

In 1900 the El Dorado Lumber Co. was formed to take over the remaining assets of the bankrupt American River Land & Lumber Co. at a sheriff's sale. The new firm abandoned the attempt to "drive" the river and switched to railroads. This change in technology was very costly since most of the original million-dollar investment in mill, chute, dam and boom could not be used. Actually only the timberlands and the small logging railroad could be used without alteration by the new firm.

D. H. McEwen was the guiding force of the new firm. He had been a West Coast and Minnesota lumberman for some years before making this purchase. He was not sole owner of the company but the extent of his interest is not known. Capital for the new firm came from San Francisco, and its president, E. N. Harmon, appeared from time to time, in swallowtail coat and derby hat, to inspect the property on behalf of other investors.

When D. H. McEwen arrived in August 1900 to take charge, his first move was to establish a mill at Pino Grande which had been a logging camp nine miles up the narrow gauge railroad from the chute. There may have already been a small mill on the site, owned by Charlie Wood, a man who had logged for the American River Land & Lumber Co. According to one report, the El Dorado Lumber Co. actually hauled out lumber for Charlie Wood from his "Barklay Saw Mill" 14 miles above Georgetown.[27] At all events, Wood was bought out and made first superintendent of the new firm. Machinery for the new mill was obtained by moving the American River Land & Lumber Co. mill up from Folsom. Construction began immediately because twenty million board feet of logs intended for the last river drive lay rotting on the ground and could be salvaged.

The first mill was rapidly expanded during the next two seasons as the problem of transporting lumber off the Divide was solved. When completed, the mill required 250,000 board feet of lumber for its construction. A local newspaper described it as very modern. In addition to the 9-foot band saw moved up from Folsom it had an 8-foot E. P. Allis band saw equipped with live rolls and "Allis & Company's largest ganged edger with a 32-foot automatic trimmer." The building was 40 by 140 feet with a green chain and transfer table over 100 feet long. The green lumber was sorted as it came down the green chain and piled on lumber cars beside the transfer table. In the building were three large boilers connected to two Allis-Chalmers Corliss steam engines with 24x48 and 22x42-inch cylinders respectively. The log canter or turner with which the sawyer rolled the log before he fed it through the saw was "a W. L. Leland of the latest design." This mill remained essentially unchanged until it was torn down in 1951.

The cableway was the key to the whole operation. The problem solved by this device, unique to West Coast logging, was simple enough. The Southern Pacific came as far as Placerville on one side of the gorge and the big trees waited quietly to be harvested on the other. The idea for the cableway is said to have come to D. H. McEwen as he sat at the bottom of the gorge that stood between the trees and their markets and looked up at its steep sides. So deep was the gorge that when finished, the cable hung 1200 feet above the river. Any railroad that tried to haul lumber down that 1200 feet and up again on the other side would be very expensive to operate. Though there were other logging cableways, none had ever tried to carry loaded railway cars across such a chasm.

Work was started on the cable in early 1901 by the California Wire Co. and was completed by July of the same year. The north terminal was situated at the top of the old chute where the railroad emerged from the woods on the edge of the American River gorge. This point soon became known as Cable Point or North Cable. South Cable

Steam tractors, hired by the season from Holt Brothers of Stockton, California, were used to haul supplies all during the construction of the cable and the railroad on the South Side. Climax No. 4, even without her smokestack, must surely have been 1902's most attractive load. Note the striping on No. 4, new from the factory. The "weather vane" on the front of the tractor helped the driver tell which way his front wheels were pointed. The Heisler, below, has just wheeled the log cars to the landing where those huge sugar pine logs can be rolled off into the pond. In the early 1900s the hills around Pino Grande still showed the scars of logging. What appears to be a valley beyond the enginehouse in the center background is due to a flaw in the negative. *(Above: Perry Baker Collection, below: Daniel O. McKellips Photo, James E. Boynton Collection)*

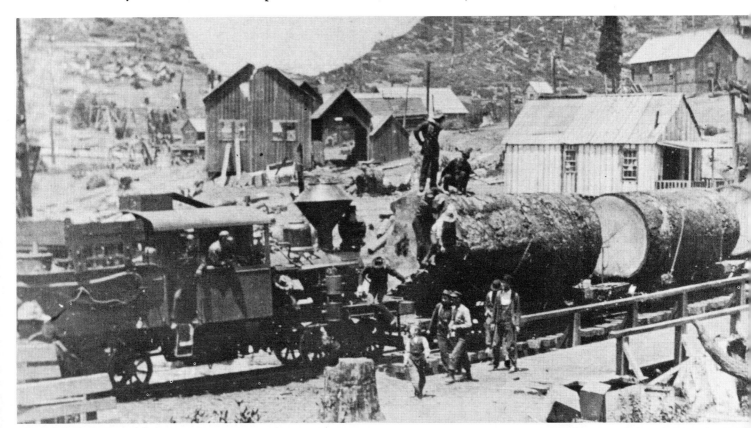

was located 2600 feet across the gorge. There work began on a narrow gauge railroad. A planing mill was temporarily set up at Placerville, but after two seasons the company moved it seven miles up the old Comstock Road, now Highway 50, to a small settlement then known, logically enough, as Seven Mile, but which now became Camino, headquarters of the El Dorado Lumber Co. and terminus of the narrow gauge railroad. Within a few years a standard gauge line was built from there to Placerville.

Supplies for the cableway and for the South Side railroad were hauled to the construction site by monstrous steam tractors, made by Holt Brothers of Stockton, California, and leased by the season. In August of 1901, a steam locomotive, Shay No. 2, arrived in Placerville and a year later a second locomotive, Climax No. 4, arrived new from the factory. Both were among the supplies taken by tractor to the railhead. There they were put to work aiding the crews which were busy laying a track of 45-pound rail. In June 1902, after the tracks from South Cable reached Camino, where 28-pound rail was used in the yards, the steam tractor stopped hauling supplies and began to haul lumber from there to the Southern Pacific depot in Placerville.

The splash dam at the foot of the old chute was sold to a certain Mr. Bell (who ultimately sold it to Pacific Gas & Electric Co.). He built a power-house farther downstream, near the mouth of Rock Creek. The first lumber cut at the new Pino Grande mill was used to build a flume to connect the dam to the powerhouse. This lumber was lowered from Cable Point to the flume on a small incline railroad that paralleled the burned and decaying remains of the old chute.

Another locomotive, Shay No. 3, arrived to help the Heisler on the North Side in 1901. It came by wagon and team from the Southern Pacific connection at Auburn. At this time the first cars to haul rough-cut lumber from the mill to the cable were built in the shops at Pino Grande. They were 4-wheel cars with approximately 7-foot wheel bases. They proved unstable and were gradually rebuilt to a shorter wheel base and used in pairs.

As soon as lumber began to be shipped from Camino in August, 1901, the characteristic pattern of sales was established, and it has not greatly changed even today. Sugar and ponderosa pine, for use in making window sash and doors, went to California and eastern mills. The latter were located in the timber belts of Wisconsin and Min-

nesota, where local supplies were exhausted. Fir and cedar were cut primarily for use by the company itself as ties, bridge timbers and stickers (the strips of wood put between layers of boards in a drying yard). Local sales were almost entirely tree tops and low grade portions of each log used for fruit boxes. At one time during these early years about forty carloads (950,000 board feet) of sugar pine were ordered by a New Jersey piano-making firm for manufacture into keys and strikers. By the summer of 1905, El Dorado Lumber Co. was so prosperous that it operated three logging camps and expanded the capacity of the mill to 225,000 board feet per day.

In 1904 the last railroad link was completed. The Placerville & Lake Tahoe standard gauge rail-road reached Placerville. This line was built to haul lumber from the drying yards and planing mill in Camino to the interchange with the Southern Pacific in Placerville replacing the steam tractors. Lake Tahoe was not part of the corporate title by accident for within one year the line was mortgaged to the California Safe Deposit & Trust Co. for twenty years, in order to raise funds for construction to Lake Tahoe. According to the newspapers, the route was to be via Pino Grande and was to use both broad and narrow gauge rails. This, however, was not likely since it would take both freight and passengers across the American River gorge on the cable or by some new grade. At this time there was constant talk of a new line across the Sierras that would break the Southern Pacific monopoly. A line through Placerville was not the only one considered; in fact, almost every pass in the Sierras enjoyed its own prospective railroad or railroads. Nothing came of this venture by the Placerville & Lake Tahoe Railroad nor of a similar proposal for a trans-Sierra railroad on the Georgetown Divide.

By 1905, El Dorado Lumber Co. had an annual output of more than 30 million board feet.* At this level of output, which became the normal annual output for successor firms, the firm was probably profitable.

Sometime in 1906 or early 1907, D. H. McEwen

Year	Production in board feet[1,28]
1901	1.5 million
1902	.8 million
1903	16.0 million
1904	20.5 million
1905	35.0 million
1906	?
1907	35.0 million

President E. N. Harmon, seated at left above, and other El Dorado Lumber Co. officers are gathered at the foot of one of the big valuable sugar pines that lured men and capital to Georgetown Divide much as gold had lured them to the Mother Lode fifty years earlier. Pine was the money crop here. The huge Douglas fir on the Pilot Creek branch, shown opposite with the picnic group beneath it, was a magnificent tree nearly eight feet through, but of little value to El Dorado Lumber Co. Fir could be shipped to Sacramento from the Columbia River in Oregon for much less than the cost of logging Georgetown Divide. Here the native fir was used only for ties and bridge timbers. The overview of Camino, below, shows the mills at center left and the drying yards and enginehouse, in the center, when all were very new in the early 1900s. *(Above and opposite: R. L. Smirle Collection; below: Michigan-California Lumber Co. Collection)*

left El Dorado Lumber Co. to take over management of a mill in Cazadero, near the coast, north of San Francisco. He is reported to have sold his interest to California Safe Deposit & Trust for about $150,000. The figure is uncertain and the buyer may have been not the bank itself but rather persons connected with it. At all events, he got out just in time, for the bank was now deeply involved in the finance of El Dorado Lumber Co. and the panic of 1907 saw them both go down. A report in December 1907 said, "Workers of El Dorado Lum- ber Co. are uneasy about the solvency of the firm since the failure of the California Safe Deposit & Trust Co. Wages are about two months in arrears. Financial panic has made collections hard for the [lumber] company who sell a lot in the East." A short time later El Dorado Lumber Co. shut down, not to reopen for four years.

Long after the panic the company remained shut down. The population of Camino fell from 500 to a half-dozen persons. Never again were the fortunes of this little lumber town to fall so low.

The little Porter 0-4-0T is shown in one of the very few pictures of the C. D. Danaher period, probably the only picture of rolling stock lettered for that firm. The typical and attractive logging camp is probably the one on Pilot Creek, when the firm was the C. D. Danaher Pine Co. (*Above: R. H. McFarland Photo, Douglas Richter Collection; below: University of California Forestry Library*)

CHAPTER III

White Pine and Red Ink 1911-1917

The next four years were filled with reports of the sale and reopening of the El Dorado Lumber Co. The second largest lumber firm in El Dorado County, California Door Co., with a mill and narrow gauge railroad of its own, was often involved. But, these two firms never merged. There was also a report in 1908 that one camp was open, turning out 65,000 board feet of logs per day; and another in 1908, that the box factory was operating. Again in 1908, the *American Lumberman* reported a proposed sale of the El Dorado Lumber Co. for $1,000,000, which, "if true, may help toward reimbursing the creditors of the wrecked California Safe Deposit & Trust Co." There was little substance in any of these reports. The prolonged idleness of the firm was due, in part, to the fact that its timber holdings were inadequate and, in part, to the depressed condition of the lumber industry.

The El Dorado Lumber Co. had among its assets only 12,000 acres of timber holdings. Though these lands were described as "the finest sugar and yellow pine forests on the coast and almost virgin," this was not much more timberland than the original purchase made by the American River Land & Lumber Co. in 1891. Not more than 300 million board feet of logs remained on the land — only an eight- to ten-year supply. El Dorado Lumber Co. had owned options on more timber, in order to protect its large investment, but these lapsed after the crash in 1907. Furthermore, by 1911, the bulk of the timberlands on the Georgetown Divide had come into the possession of the C. A. Smith Timber Co.

Without more extensive timber holdings, and in the face of a depressed market, the El Dorado Lumber Co. was sold in 1911 at a bargain price. Superintendent Charlie Wood had a hand in arranging the purchase. Later he recalled that "You could count the men in a position to buy a timber operation of this size on one hand. I had met C. D. Danaher and asked him to come up. We spent two

weeks out there looking around and he liked what he saw. He said he would send down his timber cruisers [men who estimate the amount of timber in a tract] if I would show them around. They came equipped with the back packs that they use up in the brush of the Northwest. I said, 'Hell, boys, you won't need those. We'll drive to the woods every day.' So we took a horse and buggy out each morning. C. D. told me later that I spoiled a perfectly good set of cruisers."

C. D. Danaher had earlier developed the mill at Fredalba in Southern California which became Brookings Lumber & Box Co. He also owned C. D. Danaher Lumber Co. of Tacoma, Washington. He now bought the El Dorado Lumber Co. properties for $450,000. A newspaper account at the time says that C. D. was paying only for the timber and that the mills and railroads were just thrown in. The "throw-ins" included a sawmill, planing mill, box factory, 15 to 20 miles of logging railroad, 20 miles of lumber railroad, the cable, eight locomotives, 200 bobbie cars, 50 log cars and enough logging machinery for six crews, plus ownership of the 8-mile standard gauge Placerville & Lake Tahoe Railroad. It was C. D. Danaher who gave this line its present name, Camino, Placerville & Lake Tahoe Railroad. It was necessary to spend $45,000 more to rehabilitate the property before logging could begin.

The properties were operated under the name of C. D. Danaher Pine Co., the creation of C. D. and his brother, James Danaher, Sr. C. D.'s management of the firm was not successful and lasted only to 1915. Operations were carried on during 1912, 1913, 1914 and one month in 1915. During 1914, 24 million board feet of logs were cut, a quantity that compares favorably with the cutting of his predecessors and successors, but cutting figures for the other years are not available. It is said that he cut too much fir, a lumber which could not be sold at a price that would cover his costs.

C. D. Danaher experimented with steam bucking saws. The logs were dragged down the skidway and then bucked into 16-foot lengths near the donkey which provided steam for the saw. The experiment, which took place around Jackson Springs, was a failure, for the donkeys did not have enough power to pull in logs that were 32 or more feet long. Shay No. 9 helps fight a fire in about 1917. Forest fires were very common in the "operating area" of any logging firm, in the age of steam. Most were started by locomotives or donkey engines and were quickly put out by water pumps and hoses carried on all engines. Only occasionally did these fires get out of control and present a major threat to the timber. Often during the fall fire season, every train would be followed at some distance by a watchman whose job it was to find and put out small fires. *(Above: Pine Association of California; below: University of California Forestry Library)*

During the years from 1912 through 1915 there were many rumors that C. D. Danaher Pine Co. and C. A. Smith's unexploited timber holdings would be combined. A 1913 newspaper story noted that "In Township 12, of which Pino Grande is the center, their holdings lie almost like a checkerboard. At present the Danaher Company brings out its lumber by means of a cable. It has been hinted that the use of the cable will be discontinued in a year or so and this is taken to mean that there may be some arrangement for joint operations."

C. A. Smith did not try to buy the El Dorado Lumber Co. properties or to merge with C. D. Danaher. He was having financial difficulties at a time when depressed market conditions were causing the value of timberlands to fall. Moreover, C. A. Smith may not have been any more enthusiastic about the cableway than were Danaher or the succeeding owners. Too, those partly cutover 12,000 acres must have looked minuscule alongside his own 60,000 acres of virgin timber. Between 1909 and 1910 he made provision for a logging railroad of his own. He bought land in Sacramento just north of the Southern Pacific yards for a terminal and acquired most of the necessary rights of way from there to the town of Cool, on the Divide. This was as far as he got with his own railroad plans until 1915 when the Western Pacific considered building a branch into his timber. However, the branch was not built and C. A. Smith was destined to have no part in subsequent logging on the Georgetown Divide.

The California State Board of Forestry had nothing good to say about the logging methods of the C. D. Danaher Pine Co. "Not enough pine trees are being left to reseed and if a profitable second growth is to be secured more care must be taken to prevent the destruction of young trees and fire. Signs of waste on cutover lands are enormous. Currently, many trees are badly smashed in felling, rendering one to three logs unfit. Danaher Lumber Co. [C. D. Danaher Pine Co.] makes no pretense of practicing conservative logging, and apparently no effort is being made to secure a second crop."

All during the period of C. D. Danaher management, the lumber market remained badly depressed. It did not pick up until 1916 when the nation's railroads went on a carbuilding spree.[9] (It is easy to forget in these days of steel cars that the railroads were tremendous users of wood until well into the 1930s.)

C. D. Danaher left the firm at the end of 1915. With it he left a $300,000 debt which may have been incurred at the time of purchase rather than from operations. The firm and debt were taken over by his brother and associate, James Danaher, Sr. The latter, in turn, leased the firm to the R. E. Danaher Lumber Co., organized by his son, Ray Danaher, and a nephew, James Danaher Jr.

1916 operations were successful and the general improvement in the lumber market encouraged an early opening of the 1917 season. The ledger books for these two seasons are interesting in what they reveal about the nature of the operation. The cut for 1917 included 19 million feet of sugar pine and three million of white pine. Sales during 1917 were:

Sugar pine	7.3 million board feet
White pine	3.9 million board feet
Box lumber	9.7 million board feet
Fir and cedar	.4 million board feet

This is a characteristic pattern for Sierra firms. Fir and cedar came so cheaply by sea from Oregon and Washington that they could not be profitably logged. It was pine, especially sugar pine, that paid for railroad logging. The box lumber, 24% of total sales, was sold locally. Sales to California were 46% of the total, mostly sugar and white pine, with the remaining 30%, also pine, sold outside of California.

It should be noted that the terms "white pine" and "California white pine" were often used to refer to ponderosa pine. Sugar pine is *the* white pine and ponderosa is actually a yellow pine.

In June of 1917 C. A. Smith sold out his timberlands on Georgetown Divide to long-time Michigan lumberman, John Blodgett, who had known the Danahers in the lumber business in Michigan and who, like them, was an important investor in Booth Kelly Lumber Co. of Springfield, Oregon. In January of 1918 Blodgett merged with the Danahers to form the Michigan-California Lumber Co.

The magnificent hotel in the 1924 view above was a few miles from Pino Grande. It was built by moving the Michigan Building from the 1915 San Francisco Fair, board by board. Old timers say that the interior was beautifully appointed as befits a wealthy businessmen's retreat. It was named Deer View Lodge and there are persistent rumors that "dear" hunting could be arranged as well. Unfortunately the builder died before it was completely finished and his heirs were not interested in the project. It finally collapsed into a mountain of lumber that is still there in the 1960s. The mill at Pino Grande received its one and only beautification when the Michigan-California Lumber Co. took it over in 1918 and gave it a coat of white paint which was never repeated. *(Above: Perry Baker Collection; below: Jack Corker Collection)*

CHAPTER IV

Sugar Pine Bonanza 1918-1951

The Michigan-California Lumber Co. was formed in 1918 and unlike its predecessors has remained in business to the present time. It was formed from the C. A. Smith timber holdings and the physical plant of the C. D. Danaher Pine Co. By 1912, C. A. Smith had become one of the 10 largest private timber holders in California,[2] but he turned out to be a holder only, not an exploiter. Those of his holdings that went to form the new firm included 46,000 acres of timberlands, 9,400 acres of timber rights, and 40,000 acres of timberlands with possibly defective titles—almost 60,000 acres total, valued at $1.9 million by the new firm. The assets of the C. D. Danaher Pine Co. included a narrow gauge logging railroad that ran from the trees to the sawmill at Pino Grande; a narrow gauge lumber railroad that ran from the sawmill to and across the cable and to the Camino planing mill and box factory; about 16,000 acres[18] of timberland of which half were cutover; and all the common stock of the Camino, Placerville & Lake Tahoe Railroad, which connected Camino with the Southern Pacific at Placerville. All of these, including the C.P.&L.T. common stock, were worth very little, unless the lumber company became a success.

C. D. Danaher had paid $450,000 for this capital plant in 1911. The minutes of the Board of Directors of the new Michigan-California Lumber Co. indicate that C. D. Danaher Pine Co. was now, in 1918, paid $100,000 and its $300,000 note was assumed by the new firm. This means that the property was worth about $400,000 to the new firm, or about 20% of its total assets. James Danaher, Sr., owner of C. D. Danaher Pine Co., received 1000 shares or 5% of the new firm. The other 95% of the stock went to John Blodgett, Sr., owner of the trees.[17] He became president of the new firm with main offices in Grand Rapids, Michigan. All of the firm's assets were in Camino and on the Georgetown Divide so active management remained in the hands of the Danahers in Camino. R. E. Danaher became vice-president and man-

ager, and his associate, James Danaher, Jr., became assistant manager.

Company records show that the first 10 years were quite profitable. R. E. Danaher was able to announce by 1922 that the firm was out of debt and the net profits by 1928 were almost equal to the $2 million capital value of the firm.[21] A part of these profits was paid out as dividends to the owners, but the rest went into improvements in the property. Plans for the most important reconstruction of the plant began when the manager, R. E. Danaher, reported to the directors in 1922 that "the saw mill at Pino Grande is old . . . and the cost of manufacturing lumber higher than it should be. The output of the mill is limited by its location and the *necessity of hauling all lumber over the cable.*" The cost of hauling lumber over the cable varied between 10% and 20% of the total cost of transportation from the forest to Camino. Accordingly, as R. E. Danaher put it, "I have caused to be made investigations as to favorable locations for a new mill, box factory . . . and a new route for a logging or lumber railroad."[19]

Replacement of the cable seems to have been an important goal of each successive manager beginning with C. D. Danaher and continuing until 1928 when it was rebuilt. The first news stories about Michigan-California Lumber Co. in 1918 said that as soon as possible "some method of eliminating the expensive cable will be found."[10] By 1926 a number of surveys had been run in the attempt to find a line around the cable. These are discussed in detail in Chapter V. Each started with the assumption that the mill would continue to be located near Pino Grande. Every likely route was considered, including a line all the way down the Georgetown Divide to Folsom or Roseville or Sacramento, a distance of 60 to 80 miles, depending upon the route. Even the shortest of these, one that went down Slab Creek and crossed the American River near Cable Point on its way to Camino, was expensive to build, and had adverse grades up to 3.5%. In spite of these extensive studies, the

These two pictures from the 1920s show how two of the many trestles, for which the line was famous, were built *(Jack Corker Photos)*

mill was left essentially unchanged, and the cable, though rebuilt in 1928, continued in use until it was destroyed in 1949.

The 1928 rebuilding of the cable, and related projects, cost about $700,000. It was entirely rebuilt with new towers, four carrier cables, electric instead of steam power, and a new, larger carriage. The new carriage made possible the use of an 8-wheel, skeleton lumber car with twice the capacity of the old bobbie cars. Among the related projects were several changes of grade between the cable and Camino. The pull from South Cable through Red Cut to the first summit had always been a major problem. It is variously described as 7% or 9%, but was probably closer to the former. This portion of the line was relocated to reduce the adverse grade to around 3%, at a cost of about $260,000.[23] In addition, the dry kilns were moved to Pino Grande and the planing mill and box factory at Camino was completely remodeled. These changes were all accomplished in 1928, but it took until June of 1930 to get the new cable operating properly. Each time it was shut down for adjustments, the Pino Grande mill shut down also because it ran out of empty cars on which to load the lumber coming off the green chain, the conveyor that brought the freshly sawn green lumber out of the mill to the loading dock where it was sorted and put on railroad cars. Claims for losses incurred as a result of these shutdowns mounted to more than $100,000.

Along with all the changes in mill, railroad, and cable, it was decided to put the company on a sustained yield basis. In fact, the desire for a sustained yield was one of the key factors that determined the capacity of the new cable and of the rebuilt mills. By then the company owned 78,000 acres of timber, all located on the Georgetown Divide. These holdings included several new timber purchases, one of which was a $250,000 block bought from Swiss Timber Co. of Oregon. Virgin forest still grew on 62,000 acres of the holdings; second growth was well established on the cut-over lands and the natural growing conditions would permit a complete crop rotation in from 60 to 70 years. To encourage second growth as cutting proceeded, trees 22 inches in diameter and less had been left to supply seed. After the larger trees were cut, these trees grew rapidly because of the additional sunshine and moisture available to them. Little was lost in leaving trees of this small size, because they were relatively expensive to log.

Fir and cedar were usually left because they could not be marketed at a price that would cover logging costs. Not until the 1950s did fir prices rise to the point where any appreciable quantity was sold.

The problem was to make the timber on the virgin lands last until the second growth was ready. The 62,000 acres of virgin forest were estimated to hold 1.6 billion board feet of merchantable timber. At 30 to 40 million feet per year, this would last 40 to 50 years and there were sufficient national forest timberlands near the Pino Grande mill for at least 15 additional years. Rights to cut on National Forest land are auctioned off periodically. Thus, an annual cut of 30 to 40 million feet was consistent with a sustained yield from these wonderful pine forests, and the mills and cable were designed accordingly.

After the numerous mechanical failures of the new cable were all remedied by the middle of 1930, the firm cut timber and made lumber for 20 years, without many events of note. Sometimes in the 1930s business was very slow and one old logger remembers a season in which he worked only 50 days to make only $250 for the season. However the overall profits between 1930 and 1950 remained good.

In 1933, the Michigan-California Lumber Co. gave 2600 acres of timberland on the Georgetown Divide to the University of California for an experimental, second-growth forest, which was named Blodgett Forest.

In August of 1938, the California-Nevada Railroad Historical Society sponsored a fan trip from Camino to South Cable. Approximately 300 members and other fans took the train pulled by a couple of Ten Wheelers, one of which was S.P. No. 2336, from Oakland. They arrived in Placerville at about 1:00 p.m., after a stop at Diamond Springs a few miles southwest of Placerville, where the Diamond & Caldor narrow gauge logging railroad was inspected. Citizens of Camino met them in Placerville and took them by automobile to Camino to board some lumber cars specially modified for the narrow gauge trip to the cable. Planks had been laid lengthwise on each car to make a deck and a bench down the middle. These benches were filled to overflowing with fans and the overflow rode on the pilot, tender, and cab of the locomotives. Locomotive No. 7 pulled the train and old No. 2 went along for pictures. The carriage was run across with a carload of lumber for the benefit of spectators and photographers. The train

Railfans had an excellent opportunity to inspect South Tower and see the cable in operation on Sunday, August 21, 1938. This was the one and only famous and frightening fan trip on the narrow gauge. Shay No. 7 pulled a long train of overcrowded cars across thirty trestles between Camino and the cable, while management held its breath. No fans fell off the train and the next day the management went back to the less hazardous business of logging. The picture opposite shows how the scrappers left Pino Grande! The concrete doorways in the left center used to be the front wall of the dry kilns. The brow log is visible just above the left end of the wall in the 1961 photograph by the author. *(Above: Perry Baker Collection; below: Russ Ahrnke Photo)*

returned to Camino in the late afternoon and the good citizens of Camino took everyone back to Placerville, where the fans left at 7:00 p.m. for Oakland on their Southern Pacific special train.

In the early 1940s, the company started to build what would have been the last major spur, south and west out of Pino Grande into Whaler Creek. After several miles had been graded, company plans were changed and a truck road was built instead. Federal funds were used in part to build the road. These funds were made available under a World War II law, designed to encourage the building of access roads into timber. Michigan-California had used trucks to bring timber to the railhead in Camp 15, but now, for the first time, trucks were used to bring the logs all the way to the Pino Grande mill.

By 1949 this mill was nearing the end of its active life because, with the exception of the Whaler Creek tract, a few miles southwest of Pino Grande, the scene of logging was moving farther and farther east. The haul to Pino Grande was becoming longer and longer. Serious speculation about a new mill had begun in 1939; in 1946 the general manager was authorized[20] to prepare, as soon as possible, plans for a new mill to be built at Camino or at Riverton, to the east on Highway 50. Replacement of the Pino Grande mill came somewhat sooner than expected. On March 17, 1949, at 7:45 p.m. in the midst of a storm, a fire was discovered at the South Tower of the cable. By the time an inspection party arrived at South Cable by track auto, the tower itself was com-

pletely burned, the cables all parted, and the carriage lying at the bottom of the gorge.

The cable was not to be rebuilt; this was decided almost at once. The lumber company and the county road department rushed to put the road through Chili Bar into shape for lumber trucks. Special loading and unloading facilities for trucks were installed at Camino and Pino Grande. The resulting truck haul was twice as long as the railroad haul and much more expensive, but the 1949 season went forward anyway.

A new rough-cut mill at Camino was begun in 1950 and the railroad to the cable was torn out on both sides of the gorge. After the new mill was finished in 1951, the logging part of the railroad was dismantled and the Pino Grande mill razed. Steam was gone, probably forever, from the woods.

All of the locomotives on the North Side were cut up at Pino Grande. All of the South Side engines, except Shay No. 2 and the two small rod engines, No. 6 and No. 11, were scrapped at Camino. Shay No. 5 was the last to go. It sat for many months on a short section of track, beside Highway 50, waiting for a buyer at $500. It would find many buyers at that price today.

The North Tower remained for another six years and then it, too, was swept away by a fire. But today, even without the towers and cables, it is an exciting experience to stand on one side of the gorge and look across; to look down to the American River, tiny in the depth of the gorge, and to imagine the carriage with its heavy load of green lumber, swaying slowly across.

The company's snowplow, which came from Hobart Mills, is shown above at Pino Grande. A train of cabins winds through the woods toward a new campsite for loggers. Note that an idler car had to be used between each logging car. (*Above: Michigan-California Lumber Co. Collection; below: Jack Butts Photo*)

CHAPTER V

Steam in the Forest

A mild climate and 40 to 45 inches of rainfall each year make the Georgetown Divide the ideal area for rapid growth of sugar and ponderosa pines. The pine belt of the Sierras runs north and south of this divide for a few hundred miles in each direction. The logging methods, particularly the logging railroad used by the Michigan-California Lumber Co. were used, with minor variations, by literally dozens of other lumber companies in the area. It seems probable that in these rough mountains without large rivers, successful logging had to be railroad logging and only the valuable sugar pine could pay for the railroads. With some exceptions, big scale railroad logging in this area began in the 1890s and lasted until the Diesel trucks took over in the late 1940s.

The Logging Camp and Crew

The loggers lived in temporary camps among the trees. The Michigan-California Lumber Co. operated one and sometimes two camps each season. They were opened each spring, as soon as the snow began to recede, and stayed open in the fall until the threat of snow became too great—usually May to November. Most logging by this firm was done at altitudes between 3500 and 6000 feet; at these elevations winter snows are very heavy in the Sierra. Occasionally a late spring snowstorm would oblige the firm to get out its snowplow.

One camp would house about 160 men, including 12 logging crews; six donkey engine crews; a grade crew, bridge crew and steel gang (track workers); one or more railroad crews; and a compliment of cooks, timekeepers and other service personnel. Two men were left in camp each winter to watch the property and to keep snow from caving in the roofs of the buildings. A camp might remain in one location from three to five seasons while the adjacent area was logged off. A list of the logging camps of the Michigan-California Lumber Co. and its predecessors will be found in the Appendix.

Some of the camps only could be reached by the railroad. Loggers used to drive their automobiles into Camp 9 over the railroad. The wheels would just straddle the two rails, bumping along over the ends of the ties on either side.

Loggers who were not permanent residents of Camino or Placerville were recruited each spring in Sacramento near the levee. Each carrying his own "balloon" or bundle of belongings tied up in a blanket, the men crowded around company wagons or trucks waiting for the woods bosses to pick their crews. Such gatherings must have occurred each spring in every major town in California's Central Valley.

Many of the men would stop in Placerville for a last fling, arriving at Camino in the wee hours of the morning in no condition to swing an axe. To get these "basket cases" safely to camp, a special car was rigged with sideboards; a car normally used to haul in livestock, mostly pigs to be fed on garbage and slaughtered for the cookhouse tables, and called the "hog car." Sometimes new employees never got any closer to camp than the cable, where they declined to go across. The menace of falling timber, apparently, was nothing in comparison with the seeming peril of dangling from steel cables swinging 1200 feet above the chasm.

Challengers of Pino Grande's baseball team, during the 1920s, were more determined. During the summer visiting teams from Placerville or Camino would arrive, still a little shaky from the ride on the cable, but ready for the game.

A tree falling crew consisted of two fallers, a limber and four buckers. Two such crews were assigned to each steam donkey. The fallers would chop down enough trees to average 35 to 40 thousand board feet of logs per day. The introduction of chainsaws in the early 1940s increased this output to 150,000 feet per day. Buckers cut the logs into 16-foot lengths, although fir logs were sometimes left in longer lengths for use as bridge timbers.

Two logs have just entered the Pino Grande pond, in the upper picture, from the chute that brought them down from nearby Camp 3. The steam donkey pulled them down the chute, usually several at a time, by means of a cable attached to the last log. A man would ride the string of logs as they moved toward the pond and reported any snags on a signal line that ran along the chute. A full donkey crew is shown below. Boss of the crew was hook tender Octave Laurin, second from right, one of the many French Canadian employees of Michigan-California Lumber Co. Youngest of the crew was whistle punk Clarence Pratt, the boy near the center. (*Left: R. L. Smirle Collection; below: Pete Boromini Collection*)

Logs were pulled out of the woods by Dolbeer donkeys, powerful steam engines named for their inventor, with a spool that wound in a cable tied to a log. If this cable was fastened to a stump they could pull themselves on skids up a hillside to a location suitable for operation. Sometimes they were used in tandem to increase the radius which could be logged from one setting. Eventually the early Dolbeers were replaced by two-spool donkey engines which could wind up a lighter line that pulled the main cable back into the woods after a log had been unloaded from it. This haul-back line eliminated the need for the line horse, an animal which had formerly performed this task.

Boss of the donkey crew was the hook tender, whose wife got free board at the cookhouse. On the crew were two loaders, an unhooker, two choker setters, a rigger, a whistle punk and a watchman who slept by the donkey at night and fired it up in the morning.

The loaders and unhooker worked at the landing where the logs were put on railroad cars. The choker setters put a loop of cable, the "choker," around one end of the log and fastened it to the main line from the donkey. As the log was pulled in it would thrash about violently, destroying much young growth and when it snagged on a stump the donkey had to be stopped quickly before the taut line parted. A cable parting under tension could present a considerable hazard to the life and limb of anyone nearby.

Communication between the logging foreman in the woods and the engineer of the steam donkey was provided by the whistle punk. This was a boy, usually on his first lumbering job, who followed the logging foreman into the woods dragging a light line that was attached to the whistle on the donkey. When the foreman wanted a log pulled in, the punk would give the signal by pulling on his long whistle cord. There had to be a complex system of whistle signals to make possible the prompt and proper application of power to the long cables; the whistle punk had to be an alert and accurate young man for mistakes on his part could imperil many workers with such things as falling logs and flailing parted cables.

In the early 1900s there was a fine stand of timber near Pino Grande just up Slab Creek from the mill. A camp, later called Camp 3, was built here and a chute was put down from the camp, along the creek, directly into the pond. Logs were dragged to the head of the chute by teams using "Michigan wheels," 12 to 15 feet high. These straddled one end of the log which was chained to the tongue; as they were pulled they raised one end of the log off the ground. Several logs were placed in the chute at once. Since the chute was not steep enough to operate by gravity, the logs were dragged down it by a cable from a donkey next to the pond. A man riding the logs down the chute, would jump off if they became snagged and would warn the donkey operator using a signal line beside the chute.

This technique was known as ground logging. After World War I, it gave way to high-lead logging. A spar pole, as tall as possible, was set up near the landing. A line was then run through a large sheave at the top of the spar pole to a stump called a tail block near the extreme operating radius of the donkey. Most Michigan-California donkeys could bring in a log from as far as 2500 feet away. The log was fastened to this main line by chokers around one end. As the log was pulled in, a haul-back line was fed out from the donkey through the tail block. After the log was uncoupled at the landing, the haul-back line was wound in to pull the main line back into the woods. Because the main line came from the top of the spar pole, it raised one end of the logs off the ground as it pulled it in. This solved the problem of snags, but the dragging end of the log was still very destructive of younger trees, even more so than the ground logging that had preceded this technique. The main line and tail block were moved as necassary until a whole circle around the spar pole was logged off.

Getting a spar pole was probably the most exciting part of a generally exciting and dangerous business. It was the special job of the high climber. Ideally, he would find a tall tree right by the side of the railroad track. He would strip it of limbs and saw off the top—a very special hazard. He chopped and sawed the top away at a height of 100 to 200 feet above the ground. As the top began to fall he would unfasten but hold his safety belt and quickly drop down the trunk about twenty feet. Sometimes a tree would split when the top fell away and the safety belt, if still fastened, would cut the man in two. Also, if the high climber stayed too close to the top, he risked being struck by one of the branches as the top went past on its way to the ground. Finally, he had to hang on for several minutes while the trunk swayed violently.

This high climber is probably Tom Berthelot, rigging a spar pole for high-lead logging. The spar pole was as tall as possible, sometimes as high as 225 feet after it was topped. If no tall tree was handy to the landing, one would be moved in a vertical position by tightening and loosening the guy wires until it was right beside the track. (*Jack Corker Collection*)

Often the best spar pole was not located right at the railroad landing site, and had to be moved. So a 150-foot sugar pine that might be nearly four feet across at its top would be sawed off at its base and moved in a vertical position by tightening and easing guy wires. The high climber had to "set" 15 to 20 spar poles a season, that is, he had to find three or four settings for each donkey, a full-time job. Part of preparing a donkey setting was to clean up all the brush in a substantial area around it to reduce the fire hazard. Then the fire engine was loaded on the steel flatcar and brought to the setting while the brush was burned.

In the early 1930s, there was a return to ground logging with Caterpillar tractors instead of steam donkeys. The era when steam power dominated the woods was coming to an end. Soon steam locomotives would be replaced by Diesel trucks and the handsome Corliss mill engines would be replaced by electric motors. The cats were used to drag the logs to the railroad landing using logging arches. The logging arch worked on the same principle the much older Michigan wheels had used. One end of the log was pulled up into the arch between two wheels so that as the Caterpillar tractor pulled the log along, the front end was off the ground. The loading at the railroad, however, continued to be done for many years by steam donkeys with 85-foot spar poles. By 1935, Michigan-California was doing all its yarding (moving logs to the landing) with three 50-horsepower cats, one 60-horsepower cat with arch and one 60-horsepower cat with a double cable drum for yarding out of potholes. One high-lead logging outfit was kept until World War II to log out pockets too steep for the cats.

Once a section was logged off, it was leased to grazers at the ratio of about forty acres per cow. Grazing substantially reduced the fire hazard by reducing the amount of dry grass in the late summer.

The Haul to the Mill by Rail

All six donkeys and their crews could get out about sixty carloads a day. The narrow gauge cars were 26 feet long and loaded with 16-foot logs, containing about 3000 board feet of lumber. They were equipped with link-and-pin couplers and hand brakes. Before 1918, log trains had used airbrakes but maintenance was such a problem that the airbrakes were removed. The air hoses were often torn, as they caught in switches and the air line itself often was broken by falling logs during loading. In the middle of the 1930s, log cars ran on 50-pound rails, laid on 6- by 8-inch ties, 6 feet long. Curves were as high as 45 degrees and speed was about eight miles per hour. The log cars were rebuilt twice—once in 1927, when new bunks (the beams that run crosswise to the car at each truck and actually support the log) were made out of rail; and again, in 1944, after the big, three truck Shay No. 6 was brought to the North Side. At this latter time, the log cars were lengthened so that 32-foot logs could be brought to the mill. The final bucksawing into two 16-foot lengths was done at the mill by a steam saw.

A glance at the map will show what the track was like around a logging camp at the peak of railroad logging in the early 1930s. Look especially at Camps 11 and 12 and compare them with Camp 15, which was a "truck camp." At the latter camp, the logs were loaded on trucks at points near the cutting area and were hauled to the railhead. Consequently, dozens of 2- to 4-mile spurs with tight curves and frightful grades never had to be built. In a camp like Camp 12, one engine was assigned the job of collecting loaded log cars from all of the short spurs and setting out the empties. In later years, Shays No. 8 and No. 12 were often used this way. Another engine, possibly No. 9, would then make up a train of loads and start for Camp 10.

Train orders were made up each morning by the logging superintendent from his knowledge of the previous day's cutting. They consisted primarily of orders to set out a certain number of empties on each spur in the cutting area and pick up all loads. There were no passing tracks on the main line and never more than one train at a time so no meets had to be arranged. Even on the standard gauge C.P.&L.T., as a matter of fact, arrangements were only slightly more formal. The office manager ordered the empties for the mill and when the engine crew had the once-a-day train ready he signed the train orders.

How many loaded cars made a train depended upon the branch, but the number was usually between ten and twenty. For several years in the 1920s Shay No. 3 was used as a pusher to help the No. 9 get a train in from Camp 6 but double heading was not common. No caboose was ever used on a Michigan-California log train, but other logging railroads often used them. When the "Nine Spot" reached Camp 10 with its loads a meet took place with a train of empties from the mill, possibly pulled by Shay No. 15. The two engines

Fire engines were brought out into the woods whenever debris was to be burned around a new donkey setting. The picture from the 1920s, above, shows a fire engine carried on a 40-foot steel donkey car specially built to facilitate the movement of big steam donkeys from one setting to another. Trestles were a commonplace on the logging rail-roads of the Sierra Nevada. *(Above: Jack Corker Photo; below: John P. Carrick Photo)*

would exchange trains. The haul from Camp 15 to the mill was 22 miles and, from Camp 12, it was nearly the same. Camp 10 was about half this distance and so for most of its life this was a railroad camp or division point. Three trips from the woods to Camp 10, or from there to the mill, took a 10- to 12-hour day. A trip took that long because the engines had to "wood up," a process which could take an hour or more for each trip. Additional time was spent in moving the slabs out from the mill to the wooding up stations along the line. "Wooding up" was so time consuming that Michigan-California engines were ultimately converted to oil, starting with No. 15 which was an oil burner when acquired in 1944. Conversion to oil also reduced the fire hazard.

Much land on the Georgetown Divide is part of the Eldorado National Forest. When logging on such land, the company was responsible for all fires in its operating area. The operating area is a strip 200 feet wide along the railroad and around each camp and loading area, as well as the cutting area itself. A fire trail 20 to 30 feet wide was graded on the uphill side of all new logging spurs on both company and National Forest land. All the brush was cut away around steam donkey settings and burned. Often a water-tank car was stationed in camp or at a donkey setting and one was kept at the North Tower of the cable. Each locomotive was equipped with water pump and hose, as was each donkey. These precautions were very necessary, as records generally show a dozen or more fires during the latter part of a season. Most of these occurred in the operating area; steam donkeys and wood-burning locomotives were the source of most of them, but the precautions meant that most of them were put out before much damage was done. Fire was also a very serious problem on cutover land and was the greatest single hazard to second growth.

The Michigan-California, like other logging railroads, owned a number of special and interesting pieces of railroad equipment. For instance, they had one 40-foot steel flatcar, used to move donkeys and other very heavy pieces of equipment. Also, there were a number of smaller flatcars, used to haul Caterpillar tractors around the woods and into Camino for servicing in the winter. In 1938, the company bought a very attractive eight-wheel wedge-type snowplow to open up drifts in the spring. Then, too, there was a Studebaker track auto fitted up as an ambulance to take injured log-

gers to Camino in an emergency. In times of great urgency, the 18 miles between Pino Grande and Camino were covered in less than thirty minutes, including the cable crossing.

An engineer who lived in camp all summer might have his cabin set right beside a track siding, so that he could "park" his engine in front of his house each evening. His first load in the morning would be loggers with water barrels and lunches going out to the scene of the cutting.

One engineer built a washing machine that worked on steam from the locomotive blowoff valve. At the end of each day's work he would set it, like a wooden box, beside the engine, toss his coveralls in and turn on the steam. It is said to have been extremely effective, though it significantly shortened the life of a pair of coveralls.

Special mention ought to be made of the logging incline that operated for a time near Lookout Mountain. The incline was a very steep section of track that went down into a pocket of especially fine timber. Cars were dropped down the incline two or three at a time by cable, and when loaded, pulled back up. Many trees in this pocket were so large that one tree made single log loads for each car of an entire 17-car train. The incline was not, however, very economical to operate; only three donkey settings were logged from the bottom.

The number of trestles on this railroad was simply staggering and no evidence has been found that any were ever filled. For instance, on the Camp 7 branch, for which an old map still remains, there were 57. The remains of several hundred others are scattered all over Georgetown Divide. Each was insured and a new map had to be made for the insurance company each month, showing those in use currently as new spurs were completed and older ones abandoned.

It is interesting in the 1960s to look at some of the costs of logging and railroading in those days. The lumber railroad, for instance, was valued at $50,000 in 1918. Included were 18 miles of narrow gauge mountain railroad, four locomotives, Numbers 2, 5, 7 and 10, and 200 bobbie cars. What a bonanza tourist attraction that would make for anyone who could buy it today at that price! Or consider the following comparison: Shay No. 6, Michigan-California Lumber Co.'s largest locomotive, cost $3,075 in 1944, secondhand. The company's first Diesel truck, that same year, cost $10,600 new.

Unloading logs
Pino Grande

Shay No. 8 pulls the logging train on the gantlet track past the brow log over which logs will roll into the pond. The closeness of the gantlet and main tracks can be seen between the cars at the left. The water of the pond is covered by a great mass of floating bark and debris. Below and opposite are two interior views of the Pino Grande mill taken shortly after its completion in 1902. Newspapers reported it to be "of the latest design" which was a good thing, since it was not to be changed in any important way for the rest of its 50-year life. The log is loaded on the "shotgun" carriage, moved directly by the horizontal steam cylinder. To the right of the log can be seen a vertical segment of the band saw which was moved by the spoked wheel. Movement of the log and carriage was controlled by the sawyer from his position in the pit just beyond the saw in this view. On the carriage rode the log setter who operated the hooks which turned the log. The board or slab cut from the log was deposited on the live rolls at the right. Immediately overhead was the loft, shown on the opposite page, where saws were sharpened. Two of the band saws can be seen in the view; in the right foreground are racks which held the saw for sharpening. *(Above: Perry Baker Collection; two pictures: R. L. Smirle Collection)*

The Mill at Pino Grande

As the logs came into the mill, the usual practice was to pull the whole train by the landing where the logs which would float could be rolled into the pond. A large brow log was securely fastened beside the track to keep logs from hitting the track or cars as they rolled off. To bring the log cars closer to this brow log, they were switched onto a gantlet track, a second pair of rails, each a few inches to the right of its corresponding main rail. Meanwhile the locomotive, which needed more side clearance, was allowed to pass the brow log on the main rails. The "sinkers," mostly sugar pine and white fir, were then pulled to the dry landing beside the mill and unloaded on a rollway.

An endless chain pulled the floating logs directly up onto the log deck on one side of the mill. On the way in, they were washed by high-pressure water jets that encircled the log. The sinkers on the dry landing were rolled into the water (as needed) on top of a small, underwater dolly and then pulled onto the log deck on the other side of the mill. From each log deck the logs were rolled onto a carriage and shoved past a high-speed band saw that took off a slice each time until the entire log was made into boards. The saw blades had to be sharpened a couple of times a day and would have needed even more attention if the logs had not been washed of dirt as they came into the mill. Sharpening was done in a loft directly above the log deck by one of the highest paid employees of the firm.

The two band saws, one eight foot and one nine, were steam-powered as was the carriage or "shotgun," which carried the logs through the saw. Standing in a pit beside the saw blade was the man most responsible for the mill's success. He was the sawyer who decided how each log, allowing for its size and irregularities, should be cut. His decisions had to be made very quickly, for the logs moved rapidly through the saw. With his controls he could roll the log and start sawing on any side or roll it between cuts until it was a large square timber. Most of the lumber at the Michigan-California was cut into 1½" and 2" thick boards for window and door sash mills. Only sugar pine heartwood was cut to three- and four-inch thicknesses for pattern making. From the saws, the boards went on live rolls to the edgers and trimmers and then out onto the green chain. There was no drying yard at Pino Grande and so most of the green lumber was sorted directly onto lumber cars and hauled to Camino. Some of the best ponderosa pine was dried in kilns before it left Pino Grande, since this wood tends to stain if air-dried. Drying requires about one day in the kiln for each quarter-inch of thickness of the board. Especially fine loads of dried pine were often covered with canvas for the trip to Camino. Steam to run the mill was generated by burning wood chips and the steam drove two fine polished steel and brass Corliss steam engines located in the basement of the mill.

In great contrast with the rugged loads of the logging train shown on page 42 are the trim stacks of lumber fresh from the Pino Grande mill which are carried on the cars waiting on the hillside storage tracks at North Cable. One by one these cars will be carried across the river on the carriage. In the picture on the opposite page, the loads have been reassembled into another train which arrives at Camino behind a South Side engine, the three-truck Shay No. 3. (Above: Robert Hanft Photo; Opposite: Russ Ahrnke Photo.)

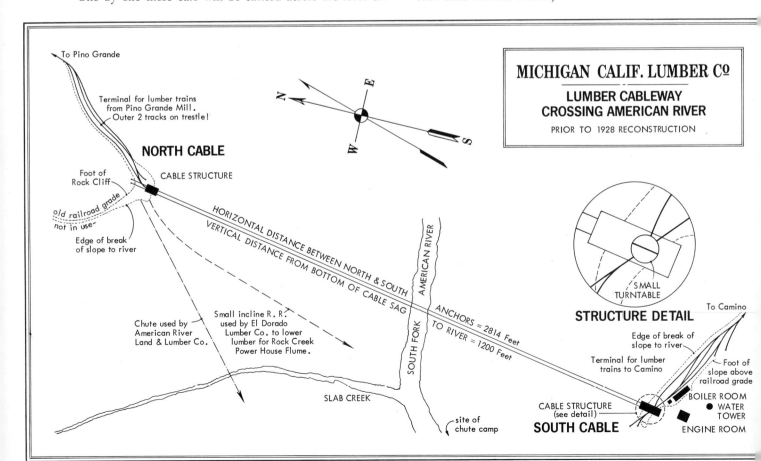

To Pino Grande

Terminal for lumber trains from Pino Grande Mill. Outer 2 tracks on trestle!

NORTH CABLE

CABLE STRUCTURE

Foot of Rock Cliff

old railroad grade not in use

Edge of break of slope to river

Chute used by American River Land & Lumber Co.

Small incline R. R. used by El Dorado Lumber Co. to lower lumber for Rock Creek Power House Flume.

HORIZONTAL DISTANCE BETWEEN NORTH & SOUTH

VERTICAL DISTANCE FROM BOTTOM OF CABLE SAG

SOUTH FORK AMERICAN RIVER

ANCHORS = 2814 Feet
TO RIVER = 1200 Feet

SLAB CREEK

site of chute camp

MICHIGAN CALIF. LUMBER CO
LUMBER CABLEWAY
CROSSING AMERICAN RIVER
PRIOR TO 1928 RECONSTRUCTION

SMALL TURNTABLE

STRUCTURE DETAIL

To Camino

Edge of break of slope to river

Terminal for lumber trains to Camino

Foot of slope above railroad grade

CABLE STRUCTURE (see detail)
SOUTH CABLE

BOILER ROOM
● WATER TOWER
ENGINE ROOM

From Pino Grande to Camino

As loaded cars came off the transfer table on each side of the green chain, they were made up into trains for the cable. About 50 to 60 carloads a day were standard during the 1920s and each carried about 2500 board feet of lumber. After 1929, when the new cable was working, 30 to 40 cars were handled per day in three trains with about 5000 board feet of lumber on each. Just before the train left the mill, two or three cars of slab wood fuel for the locomotives might be added, to be pulled to the wooding-up station and unloaded for future needs. The locomotives backed downgrade to the cable and ran forward on the return trip with the empties. Brakes were set by hand with the brakeman jumping off the train to get to the next car to be braked. On the old bobbie cars each truck had separate brakes that were set with a long pole from the top of the lumber load.

The 9-mile trip wound down a gentle grade, over about thirty trestles of which one was 105 feet high, scented with the pungent smell of green sugar pine and wood smoke. Sometimes Pino Granders liked to coast by gravity down the grade to the cable on a free-rolling bobbie car, just for the fun of it.

Loads were picked up at the South Tower by Shay No. 1 or No. 3, big three-truck engines, and pulled to Camino with one stop for water. The first part of the trip was a long, slow pull up 3% grades to Summit. Long and slow though it was, it beat the old 7%, up which the Climax used to take ten small loads per trip before 1928. At Camino, the big engine picked up its string of empties and headed once more for the cable, while old No. 2, the company's oldest Shay, began to break up the train. Dry pine was sent either to the planing mill or to the warehouse. The rest was sent to the drying yards. Each car of green lumber was permitted to roll by gravity down the long tracks between the piles of drying lumber with a brakeman to choose the stopping point. The drying lumber was carefully piled with stickers between each layer of boards and a chimney or air vent in the center. Even then it took six weeks to two months to air-dry a board one inch thick. The loads of odd length and knotty lumber that came from tops of the trees were dried and sent to the box factory to be made into "box shooks," the bundles of wood parts that would later be assembled into fruit boxes. And, ultimately, it was all loaded into a "foreign" boxcar, hauled to Placerville by the C.P.&L.T. and turned over to the Southern Pacific.

This panorama of the chasm of the American River in the early 1900s, looking west, clearly shows both towers of the original cable built by El Dorado Lumber Co. By following the line of the cables from the South Tower, beneath the puff of smoke at the left, one can pick out the carriage as a small dot, two-thirds of the way toward the north.

The prospect of building a railroad grade down one side of this canyon, across the river, and up the other steep slope is surely enough to convince most of us that the cable was necessary and likely to save money. (*R. L. Smirle Collection*)

CHAPTER VI

By Cable Over the River

The Old Cable

The cable made the Michigan-California Lumber Co. unique in Sierra logging. Other techniques might have been used to get logs off the Georgetown Divide of course. Driving the American River had been tried and had failed. A flume could have been built to the foothills where rail connection could be made. The distance was between 40 and 50 miles and construction would have been very expensive, but several flumes at least that long *were* built in the Sierras, so it was not a completely unreasonable scheme. Occasional newspaper stories mention such a flume, but none offer any information that would permit an evaluation of the project.

It was also suggested that a railroad be built down into the American River Gorge and up the other side. One source[15] has put the cost of such a line at $250,000 in the early 1900s, much more than the cost of the cable. The other outstanding alternative was to build a railroad directly down the Georgetown Divide to Folsom, Roseville or some other valley town. Several such routes were surveyed in the middle 1920s and we know that they would have cost three to four million dollars at that time. No doubt they would have cost much less in 1901 but doubtfully as little as the cable.

An article in *Scientific American* for February, 1903, gives the cost of the cable as "less than $12,000" and the Michigan-California ledgers give a value of $5,000 in 1918 when that company took over. These figures seem very low and, of course, do not include the railroads necessary to connect South Tower with the Southern Pacific at Placerville. Nevertheless, all the costs connected with the cable were probably less than the cost of a railroad down the rough terrain of the Georgetown Divide.

As originally built, the carriage ran on two cables 1-7/16 inches in diameter. The distance from railhead to railhead was 2650 feet and it was about 1200 feet from the bottom of the cable sag to the

river below. Thus, the sides of the gorge rose at roughly a 45-degree angle, providing an exciting ride then and an exciting sight even today. The cables were anchored in tunnels drilled back into the mountain on the North Side and were probably fastened to counterweights on the South Side. Each cable had a half-inch spring steel center strand and some 57 smaller strands wound around it. The usual practice, in those days, was to make the center of such a cable of manila rope instead of steel and early accounts speak of the use of cables with a steel center as experimental. They were apparently never used in another such tramway. The great weight of the cables caused them to sag about 170 feet in the middle.

The carriage rolled into a tower at each end so that loaded lumber cars could be rolled into it and clamped down for the trip across. At first, individual four-wheel lumber cars were used, but these proved to be too unstable. They can be seen in some of the earlier pictures. Very soon a change was made to pairs of four-wheel trucks which were called bobbie cars. (Such cars are sometimes called independent log buggies.) Bobbie cars continued to be used until 1928. Each pair was loaded with 2500 board feet of green lumber for the trip across. Cars of lumber were occasionally lost from the carriage. The first such accident, in May, 1902, was caused by an unevenly-piled load which slid off on the ascending portion of the cable.

There is only one report of a fatality on the cable. Bill Melchior, employed at North Cable in 1903, tells of a fellow riding the rear end of a car going across on the cage to the North Side. The car was loaded with axles. The cage stopped about fifty feet from the tower and then started again with a jerk. The axles rolled off, shoving the fellow ahead of them. "We rushed down to the rocks below. It was an awful sight."

The machinery that pulled the carriage across was originally on the North Side, but was moved to the South Side in December, 1902. Power came

On the original cable carriage the passengers rode
with the load. In the view, below, from the partly
finished original North Tower, the steep sag of the
cables which made the ride so exciting is clearly
apparent. Looking straight down from the carriage
at the river 1200 feet below, opposite, the remains
of the old chute can be seen on the right bank. The
white line on the picture is the haul-back cable.
*(Below: University of California Forestry Slide Col-
lection; two photos: R. L. Smirle Collection)*

from a steam engine, fed from wood-fired boilers, parts of which remained at the South Tower until the cable was scrapped in 1950. When the carriage came to a stop in the South Tower with a load, the bobbie car was pulled out of the tower with a horse and onto a little turntable. The horse then turned the table until it lined up with the main line and pulled the car on down the track a short distance. By 1911 the horse had been replaced with a steam winch, but the little turntable was used until the construction of the new cable in 1928. The first cableway hauled about a half billion board feet of lumber in its 25 years of existence.[30]

The Surveys

In the 1920s the cable was adding 50¢ to 80¢ per thousand board feet to the cost of transporting lumber out of the woods, about 10 to 20 per cent of the total transportation cost. Although these figures do not seem to make a strong case against the cable, in 1925 and 1926 at least six alternative surveys for standard gauge lines were made by T. O. Russell, one of the foremost logging railroad experts of his day. Three of the routes, C, D and E, came up the divide from the valley towns of Roseville, Folsom and Sacramento, respectively. Route B came from a connection with the Southern Pacific at Shingle Springs, a few miles west of Placerville. Route R went east from Pino Grande to cross the American River at Riverton, east of Camino about 15 miles on U. S. Highway 50, then back down the divide to Camino.*

The only route that received serious consideration was Route A, that came down Slab Creek and crossed the American River on a high steel bridge near Cable Point, continuing up the other side to Camino. The actual crossing was to be made downstream from the mouth of Slab Creek at the entrance of the Iowa Canyon, "the only point for miles where the river can be crossed on a tangent."[29]

T. O. Russell's comments, particularly on Route A, are very interesting. The mill site a mile northeast of Pino Grande, he said, is "admirably located with reference to the timber." It lies in an opening

---

*Costs and other statistics for the routes are listed on the following table:

Route	Cost of Construction	Maximum Grade	Length	Maximum Curve
A	$1,973,433#	4.5%	31½ miles##	20°
B	3,132,500	2.5%	53 miles	20°
C	3,775,000	2.5%	53 miles	20°
D	3,896,000	2.5%	60 miles	20°
E	4,692,000	2.5%	81 miles	20°
R	4,500,000	3.5%	72 miles	20°

#Includes cost of rehabilitation C.P.&L.T. railroad to accommodate increased traffic and heavier motive power.
##Includes the 8-mile-long C.P.&L.T. railroad.

The cable had to carry many interesting loads. Besides this track auto, it had to carry locomotives, starting with Shay No. 9 going north and the 65-ton No. 6. The steel donkey car had to be set on edge. There were also the Hobart Mills snowplow and a gas shovel that had to be suspended under the carriage, since it was just too big to ride inside. In this view it is apparent that the carriage had been lengthened since the lower picture on page 50 was taken. *(University of California Forestry Library.)*

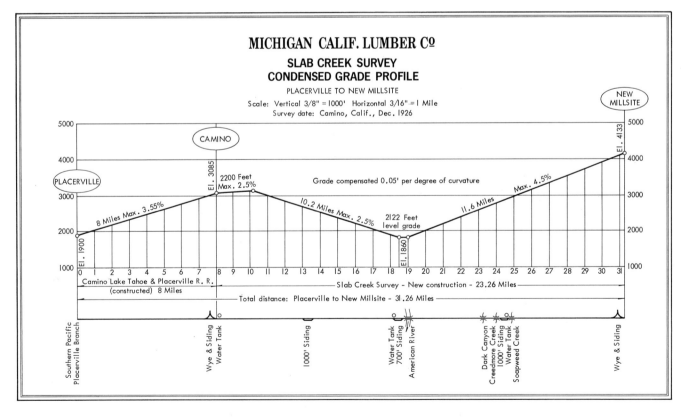

in the divide, such that "all timber from the tract must pass through it. Its use as a mill site would effectively close this opening to other interests." This gateway could be avoided by other firms only by prohibitively costly lines. "No bond house," added Russell, "would advance money for such schemes and no concern with money enough to make such a development, but must, as a *corollary* have brains sufficient to find a better investment."

The only traffic that this proposed railroad could surely count on was that produced by the lumber company. For railroads with similar traffic and terrain problems, Russell referred to the Sierra Railroad, Sonora Railroad (probably Pickering Lumber Company) and Yosemite Valley Railroad, all built as common carriers. He recommended that this road be built as a common carrier also so that the short-haul share of the freight revenues would accrue to the lumber company. However, such revenues would not be adequate to make any of the proposed routes self-sufficient. "The railroad must forever draw on the lumber company for support." If the latter cut an estimated 50 million board feet per year, it would require an average daily train of eight standard car loads. (Actually the average annual cut had been much closer to 30 million board feet.) Such a small daily traffic suggests that the shortest, cheapest line would be the best and this accounts for the fact that Route A was the only one recommended. In addition, using Route A, the train could easily make the round-trip to Placerville in a day, which would not be possible on any of the other routes.

Costs of operating the projected new route would be considerably lower, for the amount of lumber handled, than the current costs, but not enough so to equal the interest on the required investment and Russell concluded that, "considered as a unit of the lumber company, Route A will *almost* pay its way and is the only considered route that will."

Year-round operation of Route A would be possible because the west side of Slab Creek is free from snowdrift danger. There is little snow below 3,200 feet and above this point, four miles from the new mill site, there were to be no deep cuts and no high trestles; with such conditions, it was Russell's opinion "that the ordinary pilot plow will keep the line open without trouble."

Russell went on to say that he "is familiar with many of the California timber tracts, either under construction or contemplating development, and knows of none of such excellence of timber that

has been or can be so advantageously opened to railroad developments . . . none where the first cost of rail development spread to the available stumpage places so light a burden on the tract or where the haul to trunk line is shorter." However, Russell added, "the difficulty of making a more pleasing showing for standard gauge transportation argues volumes for the efficiency of the present [narrow gauge railroad and cable] organization in handling the most difficult transportation problem the writer has yet seen."

The New Cable

The most practical alternative, Route A, for lumber from mill to rail connection would require an investment of $1,973,433. To replace the cable itself would cost in 1927 only $250,000.[22] However, about $700,000 was spent at the time of the replacement because the firm also made a number of grade relocations on the South Side, rebuilt the planing mill and box factory, and moved the dry kilns to Pino Grande. At the same time, the old four-wheel bobbie cars were replaced by Pacific Car & Foundry eight-wheel lumber cars; whether this cost is included in the $700,000 is not known. If Route A, the Slab Creek line, had been chosen, this latter expense would have been avoided, since box and flatcars from other railroads would have been loaded directly at the new mill in Pino Grande. The planing mill, dry kilns, and box factory would have been rebuilt in any event since they would have had to be moved from Camino to Pino Grande. Thus, the cost of rebuilding the cable included the cable itself, the grade relocations, and the lumber cars, probably not more than $400-$500,000, or less than one-third of the cost of the proposed new line.

While these figures made it certain that the cable would not be replaced by a standard gauge railroad, the decision to rebuild the cable in 1927 and 1928 was made for another reason. In 1927, for the first time, a cable broke and sent the whole carriage crashing into the American River. This break came in the middle of the season and forced a long shutdown. During repairs, it broke again and another carriage was ruined. Jim Danaher, Jr., began to think about a four-cable model and during the winter of 1927-28, it was decided to rebuild. The new carriage was to hang on four cables, so that it would not be lost if any one of them broke.

The new cable was begun in the spring of 1928. It was located about forty feet west of the old one

When the new cable was rebuilt in 1928, Henry Ward's crew did the job. Both the old and new South Towers can be seen behind them. The little turntable was located in the opening of the old tower where the tracks seem to converge. A smokestack rises over the boilerhouse of the steam-powered cable. The extra smokestack belongs to an abandoned boiler that had never been torn out. Elaborate arrangements had to be made for anchorage and suspension of the cable, as can be seen in the construction picture of the North Tower, below. The electric motors that powered the new cable were located on the South Side at the left side of the tower itself. The picture opposite shows them soon after their installation with Bert Ybright, cable foreman at the left, and Bill Badgley. *(Below: Perry Baker Collection; two pictures: Michigan-California Lumber Co. Collection)*

and the latter was repaired so that it could be used during construction. However, so much trouble was encountered in getting the new cable in operation that the old one was used to haul lumber from the mill from August to November before being dismantled. Trouble continued all during 1929 and each time the new cable was stalled for a few hours, the Pino Grande mill had to stop, since there would be no empty cars to take the lumber coming off the green chain. Total losses from such shutdowns exceeded the gross value of the building contract with U. S. Steel and it was finally agreed by the steel company to do whatever was necessary to get the cable in operation at its own expense, if Michigan-California would drop their loss claim. It was not until June 26, 1930 that Swift Berry was able to report three months of successful operation.[16]

When the cable was being rebuilt, a complete description appeared in a lumberman's journal. U.S. Steel saw reprints of the article as good advertising and wrote Ray Danaher, then vice president of Michigan-California Lumber Co., to ask if he wanted a bunch of copies to send to friends. The letter came at a bad time, as the new cable

was out of service. Mr. Danaher replied that he did not believe he could use any of the reprints until U.S. Steel could get the cable working properly.

The contract capacity of the new cable was seventy trips per eight-hour day. The cage could travel at twenty miles per hour and slowed as it approached each tower. A trip was made in a total of 105 seconds. In practice, thirty to forty cars were taken across in a day, at the rate of nine to ten per hour. Each carried 5000 board feet of lumber and a loaded car might weigh as much as 17 tons. The maximum load for the new cable was 58,000 pounds. This should be compared with fifty to sixty smaller cars per day on the old cable, each loaded with 2500 board feet.

As before the main cables were anchored in the rocks on the north end and constant tension was maintained by four 60-ton counterweights on the south end. Ten men had been required to operate the old cable; five were needed for the new one. Conspicuous by their absence on the new cable were boilerman and fireman.

The new carriage rode on 32 grooved wheels, each 30 inches in diameter. It was 12 feet wide, 22

As construction proceeded, the old and new North Towers stood side by side, but in the distance the old South Tower is gone. The structure in the foreground was later covered by the corrugated metal building which shows in many pictures made from the South Side. *(Perry Baker Collection)*

feet high and 26 feet long, and weighed 12½ tons. Hooks engaged the axles of the cars to keep them from moving while the carriage was in transit. Passengers were supposed to ride in the little cage on top, but so much oil flew off the wheels as they rolled along that passengers were content to stand beside the loaded car and cling to the frame of the carriage. Cars were dropped onto the carriage at the north end by gravity and the empties pulled off by electric winch. On the south end, cars were moved both on and off by winch.

The usual crossing took lumber loaded on cars. However, residents on Pino Grande reported that a common entertainment for flatland guests was a ride across the gorge and many such a rider was frightened speechless 1200 feet above the river.

Coming out of the North Tower with a load, the carriage would roll off the supporting rails and start down the slope of the sagging cable. As the carriage picked up speed, one had the feeling of plunging into the bottom of the gorge, 1200 feet below. There were no fences or railings and passengers merely clung to parts of the structural-steel carriage itself. Finally, the carriage would slow down as the slack went out of the haul-back cable and then would start its steady climb up the slope into the South Tower. The trip could be especially exciting when an early spring snow threatened to coat the cables with ice or when the haul-back cable broke, as one story has it, with a party of officials on board. They got a free roller coaster ride as the carriage seesawed back and forth, gradually coming to rest at the bottom of the sag. Another exciting ride occurred when the carriage, while under repair, became wedged in the North Tower. No one realized that it was wedged until the button was pushed and everyone had climbed on to go home after the day's work. Slowly the slack was pulled out of the haul-back cable, but the carriage did not move. Then the tower itself began to feel the strain of the big electric motors pulling from the other side. It began to creak and groan and threatened to collapse into the gorge when suddenly the carriage broke free. It literally shot down the slope of the cable toward eternity, as the workmen hung, in fright, onto any available brace. Finally the carriage slowed down as it reached the upward slope of the cable and the slow steady pull into the South Tower began, but such a ride was certainly not easily forgotten by those men. The cable crew, of course, treated that wonder with nonchalance.

Generally they succeeded in getting all the cars across by 2 p.m. each day and then went fishing in Slab Creek on the North Side.

During the middle of the 1920s fame came to the cable. A young lady arrived with a parachute and several cameramen. One of her companions had a bicycle with a sling seat underneath and no tires. Balancing the wheel rims on the cable, he rode out to the middle with the young lady. There she wriggled out of the seat, pulled the rip cord on her parachute and started rapidly down the last 1,200 feet. The parachute opened about 200 feet above the river and all she suffered were scratches and bruises in the trees along the river bank. Again, about a year later cameramen arrived from Hollywood, this time, to make a dog-lover's delight called "Dog Law." An early day canine named "Strongheart" was the hero and of course a scene in which dog saves heroine from being thrown off the cable was inevitable.

Over the years several large pieces of machinery were taken across in the cable. In 1923 a large gasoline shovel was bought and transported to the other side. Its frame and treads were too wide to fit inside the carriage and, therefore, were slung underneath. The 40-foot steel flatcar (for moving steam donkeys) was also too wide and had to be set on edge inside the carriage. Even then it extended about seven feet out each end. The most impressive sight of all must have been a large Shay locomotive, loaded in the carriage and dangling over the chasm. It had to be stripped of all possible weight—trucks, engine, cab, etc. Then the boiler, the heaviest single piece, was separated from the frame, and loaded on two bobbie cars. Each bobbie car was given a 10-foot timber bolster. Then two large timbers were run lengthwise between the two bobbie cars on top of the bolsters. The smokebox rested on the bolster of the front truck and the firebox hung down between the two trucks. The brackets which usually attached the firebox to the frame rested on the two lengthwise timbers and the second bobbie car came just behind the firebox doors. When the third No. 6, a three-truck Shay of 135,000 pounds, was taken across this way around 1946, it must have taxed the capacity of the cable severely.

A fire of uncertain origin burned the South Tower on March 15, 1949 and brought an end to the cable. Glare from the fire was so intense that people in Camino thought at first that the Pino Grande mill was burning. After several attempts to call Pino Grande, an inspection party, headed

This is how passengers generally rode across! It was an exciting ride without railings or other safety devices. If one fell off, the river was 400 yards down. Once an employee crawled across the cables at night after he missed the last train to Pino Grande. He claimed afterwards that the trip was really not too dangerous because of the two cables side by side, but he added that it was a little scary.

Cable foreman Bert Ybright stands beside the carriage and load in the new South Tower to work the controls, below. The view on the opposite page shows all that remained of the power room in the South Tower after the mysterious 1949 fire that ended the life of the cable forever. (*Above: Al Phelps Photo; below: Michigan-California Lumber Co. Collection; opposite: Pete Boromini Collection*)

by Jack Berry, started out by track-auto from Camino. By the time they reached South Tower, the flames had subsided, the tower was destroyed, all the cables had parted, and the carriage was a mangled heap of scrap iron in the bottom of the gorge. The fire started in the power room, causing the haul-back cable to part first which allowed the carriage to roll out of the tower unburned. The carriage then hung at the bottom of the cable-sag until the heat of the fire caused the main cables to part.

No final determination of the cause of the fire was ever made. It may have been an electrical fire, since it started in the power room, but the main switch to the Pacific Gas & Electric Co. line was disconnected. Vandalism was unlikely, since roads to the tower were all closed by the storm and only a track auto could have reached the cable. Since no one noticed any lightning, even though the night was stormy, that explanation was also ruled out.

The mill had not been scheduled to open before May 1 because Pino Grande was still snowed in. On March 28, workmen began cleaning up the South Tower site as if to be ready for any new construction. The cost of replacement was estimated at $130,000, despite the large portions that could be salvaged. However, by April 15, the directors had decided not to rebuild. They did so, primarily, because the Pino Grande mill had only about three more seasons to operate.

By the time the mill opened in early May, arrangements had been made to truck lumber from Pino Grande to Camino on the Chili Bar road, which ran from Placerville to Pino Grande through the settlements of Chili Bar and Mosquito. Since trucks could not be brought to the green chain at Pino Grande, a transfer had to be arranged. Lumber was loaded on rail cars as usual, but these were then pushed up to a transfer crane near the road. At Camino, the lumber had to be reloaded on narrow gauge cars in order to get it to the air-drying yard and to the sorter.

The facilities for making the transfers at Camino and Pino Grande cost the company about $13,000; the company also spent about $6400 on the Chili Bar road and the county highway department spent another $15,000 before the road was suitable for lumber trucks. In addition the company bought a $6000 water truck to settle the dust on the road and still had to pay the truckers about eight dollars per thousand board feet of lumber as against five dollars per thousand for the narrow gauge railroad and cable the previous year.

Trucking from Pino Grande continued for three seasons, 1949 through 1951, while a new mill was constructed at Camino. The railroad from Pino Grande to Camino and the cable were scrapped in 1950, and the logging railroad and mill at Pino Grande in 1951. At that point one of the most remarkable logging operations of all time passed into history.

This is one of the steam monsters that hauled lumber for El Dorado Lumber Co. from Camino to the Southern Pacific railhead at Placerville before the completion in 1904 of the Placerville & Lake Tahoe Railroad. They created such a commotion that the county supervisors restricted them to back roads. Charlie Wood, lumber company superintendent, said many years later that it took many cases of whiskey to induce the farmers to sign petitions putting them back on the main roads. *(Michigan-California Lumber Co. Collection.)*

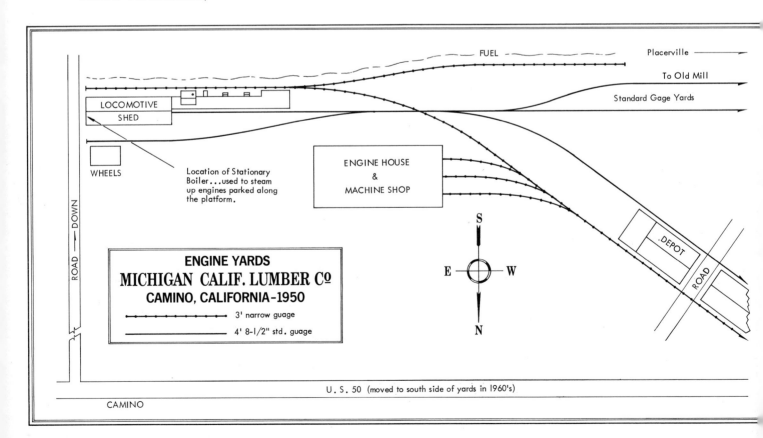

CHAPTER VII

Camino, Placerville & Lake Tahoe Railroad

Placerville, where John Studebaker began a great automotive career making wheelbarrows for miners, is the terminus of a branch of the Southern Pacific (Central Pacific) Railroad completed in 1888. The planing mill was at first located there and it appeared that a narrow gauge would be built directly from the South Tower of the cable to that city. Since Placerville is set in a narrow valley that offers little room for mills and drying yards, the planing mill was soon moved to Camino, seven miles up the road to Lake Tahoe. A box factory and dry kilns were erected in Camino and this town became the end of the narrow gauge railroad line.

At first lumber was hauled from Camino to the Southern Pacific connection at Placerville by monstrous steam tractors. One such machine could pull three or four three-wheeled wagons loaded with 10,000 board feet of lumber over the somewhat dubious roads of those days. The newspaper reported that seven wagons "will make up a train when everything is in working order," but things may never have been in sufficiently good order for that many. The tractor was hired by the season from Holt Brothers of Stockton, California, and it is doubtful that more than two machines were hired at a time. The initial trips from Camino to Placerville made with these engines in the summer of 1902 disclosed the inadequacies of the roads and "were full of incidents and accidents." Bridges had to be strengthened and on one trip, a wagon caved in an old mine tunnel that chanced to run under the road. Water pipes were reported damaged and wooden crossings destroyed. Ultimately the noise, dust and effect on teams which accompanied these machines forced them onto back roads. In spite of all their troubles, they are reported to have hauled 5.7 million board feet in the 1903 season.[6] The total cut that season was about 16 million feet, much of which was used by the lumber company itself in the construction of its own mills and railroads. In the winter, when

rain softened the roads, the tractors were put in storage and horses were used to pull the wagons to Placerville.

The use of a steam tractor was considered a temporary method of hauling lumber from the beginning. Surveys for the Placerville & Lake Tahoe Railroad were begun, in the fall of 1901, by the Southern Pacific, under contract with El Dorado Lumber Co.[5] This railroad was partly financed by California Door Co., another El Dorado County firm with its own narrow gauge logging railroad. It operated between a mill at Caldor and a connection with the Southern Pacific at Diamond Springs. California Door Co. had a big window sash and door factory in Oakland and was glad to be paid in rough-cut sugar pine lumber, according to Percy McNie, long-time Michigan-California sales manager, whose father was an officer in El Dorado Lumber Co. The survey was completed in December of 1903[7] and the contract for construction was let in March, 1904.[8] The line was completed by June 4 and freight service began in November, 1904, after a special train of Southern Pacific passenger cars was run over the line to commemorate its opening. The Southern Pacific cars proved much too long for the tight curves and the dedication trip had to be made at very low speeds. By April of 1905 the Placerville & Lake Tahoe Railroad had fitted out its own "passenger" car and begun to offer passenger service too.

Between 1908 and 1911, while El Dorado Lumber Co. was shut down, Engineer Edgar Kimble supplied an unofficial passenger service with a homemade rail car. This was probably one of the first track autos ever used. During the appropriate seasons it pulled a small flatcar loaded with the pears and apples for which the area is famous.

Excursions on Sunday to see local baseball teams in action were common in the early days, and until the automobile came the railroad offered the best way to spend a day of shopping in Placer-

Above is the depot at Camino as it appeared just before the narrow gauge was torn out in 1950. Shay No. 1, below, leaves Placerville for Camino during the 1940s. The end of steam came to the Camino, Placerville & Lake Tahoe, as it must to all railroads, in July, 1953. *(Above: Robert Brown Photo; below: Pete Boromini Collection; opposite: Michigan-California Lumber Co. Collection)*

ville. The fare was 75¢ one way and $1.25 round trip. Passenger service ended in 1936, but few passengers had been carried during the previous ten years.

As already indicated in Chapter 2 the Placerville & Lake Tahoe Railroad was intended to run to Lake Tahoe as soon as it was complete to Camino. According to the Placerville newspaper, such a line would be "the scenic road of the gorgeous West. As the shrill whistle of the locomotive, winding up and down its cloud path, shoots across glistening lake, river, heath and mountain, a chorus of echoes will proclaim another miracle of engineering and enterprise. The genius of romance will lend enchantment to the grand reality."

The enthusiasm for this plan was part of the fever of the time. At least two other sets of surveyors were in the field at the same time, one surveying for a planned electric line which would have gone through Georgetown and up the divide. All this talk ceased with the panic of 1907 which closed down the El Dorado Lumber Co. When C. D. Danaher took over the lumber company in 1911, he also took over the Placerville & Lake Tahoe Railroad and changed its name to Camino, Placerville & Lake Tahoe. The proposal to continue the line to Lake Tahoe, however, was never revived.

The road is a little over eight miles long and grades range between 2% and 5% as it climbs from 1900 feet at Placerville to 3150 feet at Camino. There were 75 curves and eight timber trestles, but most of the trestles have been filled in the last few years. There has been some grade realignment over the years, but the changes have been modest. So far as is known the road had less than 10 pieces of equipment, each of which is described in the Appendix: two Shay locomotives, two or more cabooses, a flatcar, the passenger car mentioned above and of course, since July, 1953, a Diesel locomotive. In the early years a six-cylinder

Winton track auto with water tank followed the daily train in the fall to put out fires. The engines were never turned, but backed downgrade to Placerville and ran forward with the empties on the upgrade. The trip took about three hours including switching in Placerville, and a stop for water at Blakely's Spring. Major repairs on both Shays were done by the Southern Pacific in its Sacramento shops. Before No. 2 was purchased these repairs would leave the C.P. & L.T. without a locomotive and a Southern Pacific rod engine in the 2600s or 2700s would be leased. The Shays could pull a maximum of about 18 cars, mostly empties up to Camino but the leased rod engines could not handle more than five.

Once in 1960, the Diesel and three cars loaded with 180 tons of good chips got away from the engineer; he and the crew jumped. The chip cars left the track about three quarters of a mile from Placerville. The engineer had put the locomotive in reverse, trying to stop it, and it now slowed to a stop and started back up the grade. When it got back to the spot where the crew had decided to "join the birds," the conductor, Curtis Perrce, climbed on and stopped the engine. There have been few such accidents and no fatalities in the history of the road.

As a common carrier, the Camino, Placerville & Lake Tahoe Railroad hauled any merchandise offered. Thus, at one point, many trainloads of gravel for Highway 50 went up the line. At another time, supplies and equipment used in construction of a large hydroelectric power plant on the American River were transported. During the early years, the railroad had a U. S. mail contract and during World War II, it began hauling lumber for the new mill of Placerville Lumber Co. at Smith Flat, the only intermediate station on the line. All the remaining traffic on what has become a profitable, very short line is furnished by the forests of the Georgetown Divide.

Old Pino, below, was one of the first logging camps for the American River Land & Lumber Co. Most of the buildings dated from the 1890s. This is the oldest known picture of the camp. By 1901 the scene of the logging had moved to the area around Pino Grande, but Old Pino remained an important point on the railroad, for the square tank beside the track was a watering place for locomotives, halfway between the cable and Pino Grande. In the late 1920s there was much logging in the vicinity of Camp 10, which appears in the picture above. In 1930, after the picture was made, Camp 10 became a railroad camp or division point, which it remained until 1951 when the track was torn up. A daily logging camp scene of the early 1900s appears to the right, with the teams about ready to leave camp for a day's work in the woods. During that period steam donkeys that burned slabs were gradually replacing the hay-burners. The live donkey in the left foreground bears bulging bags which probably contained water for the boilers of his mechanical name-sakes. *(Above: Jack Corker Collection; Below: Michigan-California Lumber Co. Collection; Opposite: R. L. Smirle Collection.)*

Pino Grande Album

During the transition from animal to steam power in the woods, both were used together as can be seen in the pictures opposite from El Dorado Lumber Co. times. The steam donkey is set up to pull logs down a skid road, made of logs arranged in a V shape, to the railroad landing. Timber for the mill rolled off the skid road onto a rollway and thence to the railroad cars. The horses still pulled the main cable back into the woods for the next log, and helped in the yarding. Another donkey, similar to the one on the previous page, stands beyond the stump to the left of the engine. Scenes like those on this page were common at railroad landings after the log cars had been rebuilt with "rail" bunks in 1927 and before caterpillar tractors began handling the yarding in the early 1930s. (*Opposite: R. L. Smirle Collection; This page: Jack Corker Collection.*)

The Willamette steam donkey at a landing near Camp 7, left, is rigged for high-lead logging, a practice very popular during the 1920s, but abandoned in the early 1930s as caterpillars took over the yarding of the trees from stump to railroad landing. Replacement of these donkeys began the elimination of steam from logging in the Sierra. Below, a logging crew of the 1930s heads for the woods from camp, behind Shay No. 9, to begin a day's work. Crews had lots of trouble with bears, both in camp looking for food stores, and out at the cutting area looking for the loggers' lunches. (*Jack Corker Photos.*)

This small steam donkey is probably of the type used to load log cars at a landing in the woods. These machines continued in use for loading many years after the big yarding engines had given way to the cats. This one was photographed in the 1940s. The picture from the early 1900s, below, shows sugar pine logs being rolled onto railroad cars; a partly loaded car can be seen at the end of the rollway, just in front of the two men. In the right background are a smoking locomotive and two other loaded cars. (*Right: Jack Butts Photo; Below: R. L. Smirle Collection.*)

Tracklaying was still pretty much of a job for manpower in 1922, from grading and laying steel to framing of bridge timbers. The track here is a new spur on the Camp 5 branch. By the early 1940s men had power to assist them in loading a cabin on the rail bunks of a log car. Each cabin held four men and was moved from camp to camp as the scene of logging operations shifted. Shay No. 6 will soon be ready to move a string of these cabins out of Pino Grande. *(This page: Jack Corker Collection; Opposite: Jack Butts Photos.)*

Overleaf: President E. N. Harmon of El Dorado Lumber Co. stands proudly beside the new Shay No. 5 with a six-car train of logs on the way to Pino Grande from Mutton Canyon. The engine was in beautiful, fresh-minted condition, but unfortunately soon proved too small for this work and No. 8 was brought in. *(R. L. Smirle Collection.)*

Early one fine spring morning in 1947, Photographer John P. Carrick set out with the daily logging train from the end of the line at Camp 15 to Pino Grande, recording scenes and events along the 22-mile run. The engine left the camp in the long shadows of early morning, around many curves and on an occasional straight stretch. Logs this large, one to a load, were not unusual on the Michigan-California Lumber Co., even in the last days of railroad logging. The rough-and-ready square tanks may have looked crude, but they held water.

The logging train with Photographer John Carrick aboard crossed many bridges with water barrels for fire protection. The cattle on the track had in a way the same purpose, as their grazing reduced fire hazard from grass and undergrowth during dry summers and falls; they also provided the company with revenue from grazing rights leased to local ranchers. At the lower right the train, behind Shay No. 6, rests at Camp 10, halfway from Camp 15 to Pino Grande. Here engines with logs from the woods often traded trains with engines bringing strings of empty log cars from the mill. This picture is unusual in that the engine heads toward the mill, whereas the more usual practice was for engines to go forward when headed away from Pino Grande and to back on their return. Below, the Shay takes water from the Pino Grande tank, after which the logs will be unloaded over the brow log into the pond.

Many trees on Georgetown Divide are comparable with the one which provided the entire train of logs, in the upper picture, opposite, which is pulled to the log dump by Shay No. 3. Having reached the brow log, above, the train will have to wait until the pond has cleared up a bit so that the rest of the logs can be dumped. The view across the pond below shows the two chains which bring the logs to the saws in the mill. The chain at the right brings the log from the pond; more complicated is the arrangement for the "sinkers," mostly sugar pine, at the left of the picture. Two of these can be seen on the little flatcar just being rolled into the mill. To the left of this car is the dry rollway where they were kept until needed. When the mill was ready for them the car was lowered into the water and the sinker logs rolled onto it. The lower picture, opposite, suggests that the brow log and pond had changed little over nearly two decades, but that the forest which was logged over in the early 1900s had substantially grown back by about 1920. Even more dramatic is the contrast between the desolate setting of the Pino Grande water tower in the upper picture opposite and the same tank as seen in the 1947 picture on page 76. *(Lower left: Perry Baker Collection; Three pictures: R. L. Smirle Collection.)*

At the left is another view of a log being hauled up from the pond to the band saw. In the background Heisler No. 1 can be seen at work, switching a couple of loads behind the dry landing. The inside view of the mill looks toward the opening through which the logs entered from the pond. The band saw is visible below the housing in the center. The live rolls are in the foreground and to the left is the chain that conveys the green lumber to the transfer table outside which appears below in a picture taken before the side walls of the mill were completed. All the mill operations were powered by the wonderful old Corliss type steam engines. Several were used right up to the end of the Pino Grande mill in 1951. The one shown above was an 18″ x 36″ girder type used in the box factory at Camino. (*Above: Michigan-California Lumber Co. Collection; Three pictures: R. L. Smirle Collection.*)

Green lumber emerged from the mill to be sorted and loaded onto the cars as shown in the picture to the left. The cars are drawn up on either side of the sorting platform ready to receive the lumber as assigned by the mill's expert graders. El Dorado Lumber Co.'s President Harmon, who apparently liked to have his picture taken, is standing on the left side of the platform. The picture left, below, presents an especially fine view of the whole Pino Grande operation decades later, in 1941. Brow log, pond and dam show few changes, but the once-cutover hills in the background, partly obscured by smoke and steam, show vigorously growing new forest. The sawmill building has had a number of additions. The old cars have been replaced by Pacific Car & Foundry Co. cars, some of

which are being loaded with lumber at the transfer table. Empties are lined up on the ready track just the other side of the green chain at the left center. This ready track can be seen more clearly below. The sharply curved track has one of the lumber cars on it, partly obscured by the tree at the right of this 1949 view. The view above is from the early 1900s, showing Shay No. 5 all set for a trip to the cable with a string of cars. The trestle in the upper left is on the main line to the woods. The big timbers stacked along the track are primarily fir, cut for ties and bridge timbers on the railroad. *(Above: Jack Corker Collection; Below: Robert E. Searle Photo, James M. Boynton Collection; Left: Michigan-California Lumber Co. Collection; Lower left: Russ Ahrnke Photo.)*

NO. 80 S. BAND MILL,
EL DORADO LUMBER CO.

TURRILL & MILLER PHOTO. S.F.

The 1901 view of the Pino Grande mill, upper left, is the earliest known. It was then only a single-band mill; when the machinery from Folsom was moved up a year later, it became a double-band mill and the green chain and transfer table were shifted to the left side. It appears that all the loaded cars are of the single-truck variety, which were soon to be replaced by shorter cars used in pairs, the bobbie cars. The second saw had been added by the time the picture at the left had been taken, showing the mill in full operation using both saws. The main line to the woods goes off to the left; the new south main line switchback on the hillside to the right is twenty years in the future. The old chute coming into the pond from nearby Camp 3 is visible just to the left of the mill roof. Before the United States Forest Service got particular, disposal of slash was fairly easy. Slab cars were loaded on a track just on the other side of the fire wall, above. When the Michigan-California Lumber Co. took over the operation in 1918, one of its more conspicuous moves was to paint the mill white. There is as yet no sign of the new south main line on the hillside to the left; this would be a later innovation. *(Below: Jack Corker Collection; Upper left: Michigan-California Lumber Co. Collection; Two pictures: R. L. Smirle Collection.)*

The building opposite was the first church and school at Pino Grande, serving employees and their children during the early 1900s. Teacher and pupils of the class of about '02 appear wrapped in thought. It may be surmised that the majority of the children represented a single family. Wheels on the early-day track auto—or autos—on this page could evidently be adjusted for standard gauge, although they are shown on narrow gauge rails, at South Cable, above, and on the horseshoe trestle on the first main line just outside Pino Grande. The steam Oldsmobile in the lower picture was soon discarded, as it did not have enough steaming capacity. The group above seems rather formidable for the seating capacity of the little vehicle. (*Above: Edgar Kimble Collection; Three pictures: R. L. Smirle Collection.*)

This aerial photograph was taken just before the Pino Grande mill was torn down. The switchback and the "new" south main line can be seen along the right edge of the photo. Below and to the left of the center is the transfer crane that was used to load lumber from railroad cars to trucks after the cable burned. *(Michigan-California Lumber Co. Collection.)*

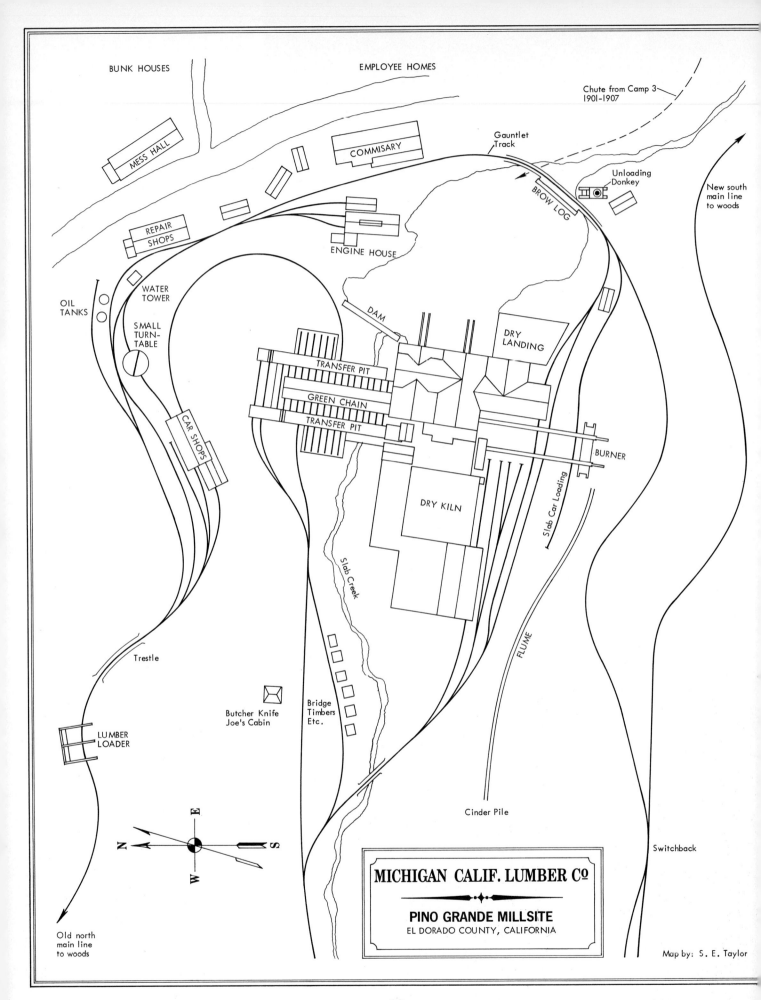

BUNK HOUSES   EMPLOYEE HOMES

Chute from Camp 3
1901-1907

MESS HALL

COMMISARY

Gauntlet
Track

Unloading
Donkey

BROW LOG

New south
main line
to woods

REPAIR
SHOPS

ENGINE HOUSE

OIL
TANKS

WATER
TOWER

SMALL
TURN-
TABLE

DAM

DRY
LANDING

TRANSFER PIT

GREEN CHAIN

TRANSFER PIT

CAR SHOPS

BURNER

DRY KILN

Slab Car Loading

Slab Creek

Trestle

FLUME

LUMBER
LOADER

Butcher Knife
Joe's Cabin

Bridge
Timbers
Etc.

Cinder Pile

Switchback

N E S W

Old north
main line
to woods

MICHIGAN CALIF. LUMBER Cº

PINO GRANDE MILLSITE
EL DORADO COUNTY, CALIFORNIA

Map by: S. E. Taylor

Shay No. 5 appears on this page in two early pictures of the lumber run from Pino Grande to the cable, and both pictures are very unlike the operations which became customary. The single-truck lumber cars were unstable and soon changed. They would run the engines forward when bringing empties to Pino Grande, and generally went backwards when hauling loads to the cable. (*Above: H. F. Dennison Photo; Below: Daniel O. McKellips Photo; both from James E. Boynton Collection.*)

Some of the routine at the North Tower during the 1940s can be observed on the page opposite. The carriage is in the tower; the empty lumber car it brought from the South Side has been drawn from the carriage by a small cable wound on the niggerhead which appears directly beyond the load of lumber in the foreground. The load will drift onto the carriage by gravity, its speed controlled by the brakeman riding behind it who has increased his leverage on the brake wheel by means of a club between the spokes. Lunchtime is at hand and the brakeman will have about eight minutes to devote to his lunch before the carriage is back from the other side with another empty to be taken to Pino Grande and ready for the next load to go to Camino. A long string of empties, below, trails behind Shay No. 4 on the way back to Pino Grande. (*Robert M. Hanft Photos.*)

Winter brought a special beauty to Pino Grande, as can be seen in this view from the porch of one of the employees' homes, taken during the 1940s, below. The mill and pond are visible at the right center. It snowed in the good old days, too. Above are two Shays bucking snow near Jackson Springs in the 1920s. Shays No. 3 and 9 are pushing the eight-wheel snowplow toward Camp 12 after a heavy spring storm, about 1938, opposite. The plow had recently been acquired from Hobart Estates, an elaborate narrow gauge logging line just north of Truckee, California. It was the first separate plow on the Michigan-California Lumber Co. roster. (Above: Jack Corker Photo; Below: Michigan-California Lumber Co. Collection; Opposite: Pete Baromini Photo.)

On the following spread: El Dorado Lumber Co.'s first brand new locomotive was Climax No. 4, which was used to haul loads of lumber up the 7% grade from South Cable to the summit. Its power can be inferred from the 21-car string of loaded single-truck lumber cars on its drawbar. The pride of the company's ever-photogenic President Harmon, who stands on the footboard, is understandable. (*R. L. Smirle Collection.*)

The routine at South Tower, the reverse of that at the other end of the cable, can be observed on these pages. A line from a small electric winch is hooked to the loaded car to pull it from the carriage and tower. As it approaches the load which preceded it across the gorge, to which it will be attached by the link-and-pin coupler, Charlie Ross, below, walks back to get an empty ready to be loaded on the carriage for the return trip. Finally, opposite, the empty is loaded on the carriage which is on its way back across the cable to the North Side, while the loaded cars here on the South Side wait for a full train to be made up. (*Above: Michigan-California Lumber Co. Collection; Two pictures: Russ Ahrnke Photos.*)

— 96 —

General Superintendent R. L. Smirle of El Dorado Lumber Co. kept this surrey to take his family to Placerville, for his wife refused to ride on the cable. The other three pictures here are from the 1940s. Below, Shay No. 3 is ready to start for Camino with the loads that have just come across the cable. Opposite, Shay No. 1, with a heavily-laden lumber train, passes through the cut at the summit and on the curved trestle near Camino. *(Above: R. L. Smirle Collection; Below: Western Pine Association; Two pictures: Al Phelps Photos.)*

Overleaf: Shay No. 5 draws a long lumber train across trestle No. 29 of the 31 that lay between Pino Grande and the cable, in the days of El Dorado Lumber Co. No caboose was used then or ever on these lumber trains. *(R. L. Smirle Collection.)*

— 101 —

The planing mill and box factory at Camino looked like this shortly after completion by El Dorado Lumber Co. From time to time the company leased the plant to other operators, as in the case of the interior view of the resaw department of the W. F. Barnes Box & Lumber Co. *(Above: R. L. Smirle Collection; Below: Michigan-California Lumber Co. Collection.)*

Shay No. 2 is a classic example of a very rare 2-cylinder Shay, dating back to 1884. It is switching in the Camino yards with engineer Tom Jinkerson at the throttle. Below, Shay No. 1, after bringing in a train of loads from the cable, helps out with the switching at Camino. *(Above: Roy F. Anderson, Jr. Photo; Below: Robert M. Hanft Photo.)*

The first motive power for the 5% grades of the Placerville & Lake Tahoe Railway was this three-truck Shay. It had been Lima's display locomotive at the Louisiana Purchase Exposition in St. Louis in 1904 and began work on the P. & L. T. as soon as the fair was over. Here it stands in brand-new splendor at Camino. For some reason President Harmon is not in the picture. Perhaps he did not wish his likeness to be associated with the string of swaybacked boxcars that contrasted so sadly with the elegance of the company's new locomotive. Little is known of the home-built passenger car of the Placerville & Lake Tahoe. Perhaps a few passengers could have been accommodated in the neatly lettered baggage and mail car at the left. *(Below: Michigan-California Lumber Co. Collection; Left: Roy D. Graves Collection.)*

Placerville & Lake Tahoe Shay No. 1 makes up a train at Camino for interchange with the Southern Pacific. Just to the right of the very middle of the picture is narrow gauge Shay No. 2 taking on oil. When this picture was taken, before 1907, No. 2 was already about twenty years old and wearing the grotesque steel cab that went unchanged until the 1940s, when it was replaced by the more comely one shown in the portrait on page 105. In the picture below is the landing dock where lumber was transferred from the narrow gauge cars to standard gauge cars of the P. & L. T. or to the dry kilns. *(Both: R. L. Smirle Collection.)*

The enginehouse at Camino burned in 1913 with the sad results shown above. The engines are, left to right, Shay No. 7 and Shay No. 2, both of which survived. Not so fortunate was the locomotive at the right which had been leased from the Diamond & Caldor Railroad. The aerial view of the Camino Mill complex was taken in 1950, after the cable had burned and before construction was begun on the new rough cut mill to replace Pino Grande. The new mill, including dry kilns, used up the entire drying yard, while the complex of buildings in the lower left remained essentially unchanged. The engine yard is at the lower right. *(Above: Edgar Kimble Collection; Below: Michigan-California Lumber Co. Collection.)*

The great 1938 excursion which brought railfans over the narrow gauge and all the way to the cable has been described and pictured on pages 33 to 35. The Camino, Placerville & Lake Tahoe ran a number of later excursions, the first of which was in November, 1951. The informality of the 1938 occasion is suggested in the upper scene, opposite, with fans seated on a lumber car behind Shay No. 7 while Shay No. 2, along for the pictures, watered up. The high festivity of the occasion is further exemplified in the scene below at the Southern Pacific station in Placerville, where a band is on hand to serenade the visitors as they prepare to leave for Oakland and home. More businesslike, apparently, was the 1951 excursion shown in Placerville, with fans securely encased in massive Harriman coaches and, as appears in the lower picture, opposite, in a steel gondola car. Shay No. 1 still retains much of the handsome dignity which Lima had proudly exhibited to the world. *(Above: Al Phelps Photo; Below: Perry Baker Collection; Opposite above: John R. Cummings Photo; Opposite below: J. F. Corker Collection.)*

Shay No. 2 stops for water part way up the 5% grade from Placerville to Camino, at the left. Above, the same engine draws a single boxcar and caboose toward Camino in October, 1949. Diesel No. 101 was so light that regulations permitted the company to use one man in the cab, provided no caboose was on the train, and since then none has been needed on the Camino, Placerville & Lake Tahoe. In 1955 Shay No. 2 was given to Traveltown, Griffith Park, Los Angeles. It and its tender were loaded on flatcars at Camino, left above, awaiting their trip to Southern California. *(Above: Al Phelps Photo; Three pictures: Michigan-California Lumber Co. Collection.)*

Appendix A

LOGGING CAMPS OF MICHIGAN-CALIFORNIA LUMBER CO. AND ITS PREDECESSOR COMPANIES
(This list is as accurate as the memories of the old loggers can make it.)

American River Land & Lumber Co.

1891-1901	Chute Camp	Used in construction of the chute and later the cable; never used as a logging camp.
1893-1912	Camp 4	Later called Old Pino.
1896?-1901	Pino Grande	This ceased to be a logging camp in 1901 when it became the site of the sawmill which remained here until 1951.
1896-1900?	Gaddis Creek Camp	

El Dorado Lumber Co.

1901- ?	Mutton Canyon Camp	
1901-1912?	Old Camp	
1901-1913?	Camp 3	On Slab Creek just upstream from Pino Grande. Logs were brought to the mill down a chute that shows clearly in early photos.

C. D. Danaher Pine Co.

1913-1921+	Camp 1	At Jackson Springs where a number of camps were built at different times.
Open in 1916	Camp 2	At Butcher Corral (near small slaughter house used by rancher).
1917?-1921	Camp 4	At Jackson Springs.

Michigan-California Lumber Co.

1919-1925	Camp 5	
1923-1927	Camp 6	
1924-1928	Camp 7	
1927	Camp 8	
1928-1929	Camp 9	
1928-1930	Camp 10	After 1930 Camp 10 became a railroad camp that was used until 1950.
1929-1934	Camp 11	
1934-1936	Camp 12	Near Uncle Tom's Cabin, a hamlet old and famous with fishermen.
1936?-1939	Camp 14	This became a railroad camp after Camp 15 was opened.
1939-1951	Camp 15	

Appendix B

LOCOMOTIVES OF MICHIGAN-CALIFORNIA LUMBER CO.
AND ITS PREDECESSOR COMPANIES

The Michigan-California Lumber Co. and its predecessors had a total of 21 locomotives. Most were Shays, the most successful logging locomotive in the Sierras, but the roster also included a Heisler, a Climax, three small rod engines and a small gasoline locomotive. The notes on the history and use of these engines which follow were gleaned from the memories of retired locomotive engineers: Pete Boromini, Jack Williams and Tom Jinkerson. Most of the statistical data were provided by R. D. Ranger and Douglas S. Richter.

The locomotives are listed, as nearly as possible, in order of their purchase. The exception may be the enigmatic Porter (or Porters), listed as No. 6.

This special casting was designed by Superintendent Smirle to hold the bearings of the main crankshaft, which tended to break on Shay No. 8 when it first arrived. The casting became standard on Shay locomotives. (*R. L. Smirle Collection.*)

No. 1
Heisler 2T   Heisler #1014   Built 1898
Weight 50,000   Cylinders 12½ x 12   Drivers 33"
Boiler pressure 160   Tractive effort 10,500
[An engine acquired in 1942 became the
Second No. 1]

Heisler No. 1 was probably the second locomotive of the American River Land & Lumber Co., despite the number. It seems to have been ordered in 1892 and was the 14th Heisler built by the firm then known as Stearns Manufacturing Co. Long before it arrived the lumber company had bought a Porter dinkey that has the distinction of being the first locomotive to enter the forested stillness of Georgetown Divide. This 0-4-0 will be discussed under Engine No. 6. The Heisler arrived by flatcar in Folsom and was transported by team and wagon to the railhead at Pino Grande. In October of 1898 it was set up and operat-ing[11] just in time for the last logging done by American River Land & Lumber Co. During these early years its number was 2; the Porter #1389, described below as No. 6, would have been No. 1. Two photos taken before 1900 show a number 2 on this Heisler's boiler front number plate. In about 1900 the Porter was sold and this Heisler was redesignated No. 1. The Heisler's busiest years were between 1900 and 1907 when El Dorado Lumber Co. took over and began the techniques that would make logging on the divide successful. Number 1 pulled the first logs into the mill at Pino Grande and later assisted Shays No. 3 and No. 8 with log hauling and switching around the mill. The first stage of retirement began after Shay No. 9 came from Lima in 1913, when the Heisler was assigned to the track-laying crews that were continu-ously pushing some new spur out into virgin timber. Finally in 1930 the "One Spot" went into permanent retirement on a little-used spur in Pino Grande and there it sat until it was cut up for scrap in 1942.

No. 2

Shay 2C2T   Lima #122   Built 1884

Weight 46,000

Cylinders 10 x 8   Drivers 24″ (26″ when new)

Boiler pressure 180   Tractive effort 13,000

Number 2 seems to have been the first locomotive on the South Side. The Placerville paper reports[4] the arrival of a narrow gauge locomotive, probably No. 2, for the "El Dorado Lumber Co. road betwen Placerville and Chute Camp" in August 1901. As the pictures testify, this is a very old, wizened and thoroughly delightful two-cylinder Shay which is fortunately still alive and may run again. It was bought from the Rumsey Lumber Co. of Big Rapids, Michigan. First and always, No. 2 was the switch engine in the yards at Camino, with Tom Jinkerson as engineer from about 1906 until the narrow gauge was abandoned in 1951. Since then it has rested on a short display track in Camino, though there was some talk a few years ago that it would go to the Smithsonian Institution as the oldest Shay locomotive in use at the time of its retirement and possibly the oldest Shay in existence. It is now likely to stay in Camino and maybe even to operate on a portion of the old line which is being rebuilt by the Camino, Cable & Northern, a tourist railroad which opened in 1965.

Heisler No. 1 had been retired on a back track at Pino Grande for over a decade when its portrait was made, opposite. Below, Engineer Jinkerson sits at the throttle of the engine he ran for many years. *(Two photos: Russ Ahrnke.)*

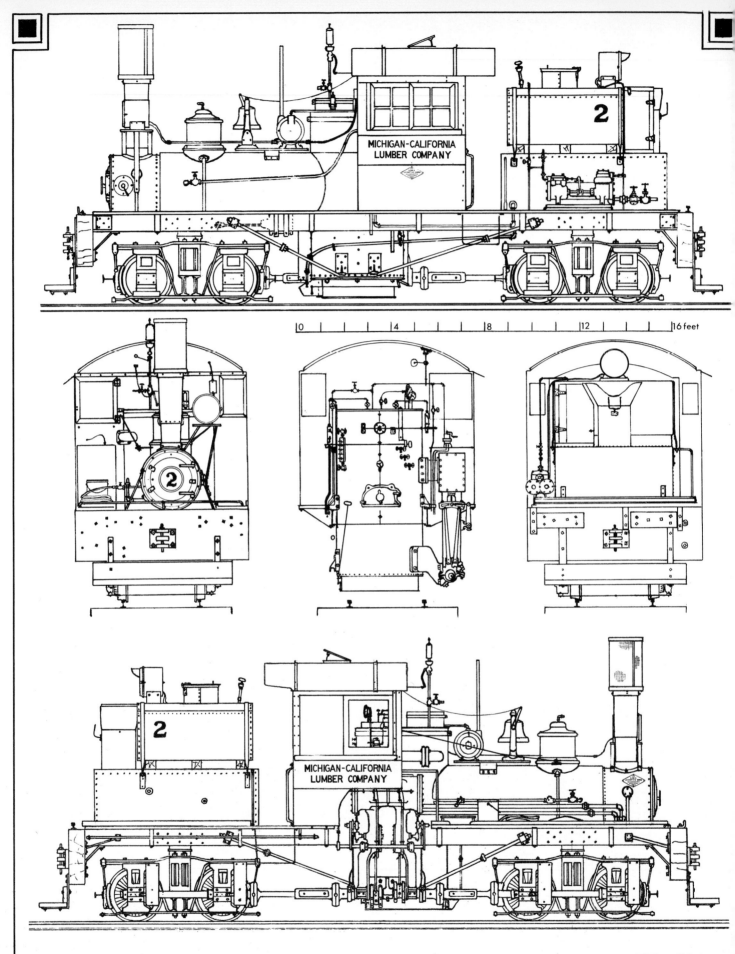

0   4   8   12   16 feet

NARROW GAUGE SHAY NO. 2 · MICHIGAN-CALIFORNIA LUMBER COMPANY · BUILT 1884

MEASURED & DRAWN in 1951 by CLIFFORD D. GRANDT

Before the late 1930s Shay No. 2 had to live with the very grotesque sheet metal cab shown below. At the time it retired from active service in 1951, with a more comely cab, it was believed to be the oldest Shay in service, so it was placed on the display track by the company offices in Camino, where it slumbers in the upper picture. It may well be the oldest Shay still in existence. *(Above: Cliff Grandt Photo; Below: Douglas Richter Photo.)*

No. 3
Shay 3C2T   Lima #159   Built 1886
Weight 41,100   Shipped 10/14/86
Cylinders 10 x 10   Drivers 28″
Boiler pressure 160   Tractive effort 13,000
[An engine acquired in 1939 became the
Second No. 3]

Number 3 seems to have been hauled through Georgetown to Pino Grande by teams in September, 1901. Like No. 2 it came from Michigan, from the lumbering firm of Blodgett & Byrne. This is the same Blodgett who 17 years later formed Michigan-California Lumber Co. There is a persistent story that it served on the South Side for a very brief period in 1901, however, most of its life was spent on the North Side, first as a logging engine and then on the lumber run to the cable. Number 3 died in harness in 1929 when a large tree twisted as it was being felled and landed on top of the boiler. It never ran again, but sat forlornly on a siding at Pino Grande for many years. The last known photograph was taken in 1937 but the exact date when it was scrapped is not known.

By the time Shay No. 3 had this picture taken, the graceful fluting that once adorned its steam dome was gone. The man on the boiler does not seem to find his perch a hot seat. *(Pete Boromini Collection.)*

No. 4

Climax 2T	Climax #339	Built 1902
Weight 67,000		Cylinders 12 x 14
Drivers 31″		Boiler pressure 160

[An engine acquired in 1940 became the Second No. 4]

This was the first new engine bought by El Dorado Lumber Co. It was, by the testimony of engineers still alive, very powerful and was used to pull loads up the 7% grade from South Cable to the first summit. In fact, it may have been bought precisely for this purpose and it continued to be used this way until C. D. Danaher replaced it with No. 10 in 1913. Three years later the Climax was taken apart and carried across on the cable. During the crossing one truck was spilled off the carriage into the American River and another had to be ordered. On the North Side it was used for unloading at Pino Grande landing, then for switching in the camps and finally as the locomotive for the steel gang, the rail-laying crew. It was very slow, making some six miles per hour, and seemed likely to shake itself apart even at this low speed. Number 4 retired in the early 1930s and sat with the Heisler for several years on a siding in Pino Grande. Unlike the Heisler, however, it was reconditioned and used for a short time in the late 1930s. It retired again in 1939 and was finally cut up along with the Heisler in 1942.

The powerful little Climax No. 4, spark-arresting screen atilt, stands cold but well supplied with slab wood by the cabin of engineer Pete Boromini at Camp 10 in this 1939 view. The engineers, with the benefit of portable company cabins and the inherent mobility of locomotives, had a big advantage in convenience over many of the employees in the woods, who often had to live miles from where they worked. *(Al Phelps Photo.)*

No. 5

Shay 3C2T	Lima #797	Built 1903
Weight 52,150	Shipped 6/5/03	
Cylinders 9 x 8	Drivers 26½″	
Boiler pressure 160	Tractive effort 9150	

Shay No. 5 was also new when El Dorado Lumber Co. bought it, and was almost certainly hauled into Pino Grande by wagon. It was used on logging trains until No. 8 came in 1906, and then was used on the lumber run from Pino Grande to the cable. When the new lumber cars were bought in 1928, No. 5 proved too light for the lumber run and was given the job of unloading at the Pino Grande landing. In 1947 it was taken apart and brought across the cable to the South Side. A 12-inch section was cut out of the middle of the tender to give better visibility and the No. 5 assumed switching duties around Camino. In 1951 after the narrow gauge was all gone, it sat for some time on a small section of track in Camino waiting for a buyer. Number 5 finally got the torch in 1953, the last Michigan-California locomotive to be scrapped.

After it was taken off the logging run, Shay No. 5 plugged away on the chores around Pino Grande, as in this view. Porter No. 6 may have been handsome in the bloom of youth, but shows little loveliness in the 1940 view on the other page. *(Below: Al Phelps Photo; Opposite: Russ Ahrnke Photo.)*

No. 6

0-4-OT	Porter #1389	Cylinders 9 x 14
Built 1892	0-4-OT	Porter #2049
Cylinders 7 x 12	Built 1899	Weight 16,000

[An engine acquired in 1934 became the
Second No. 6;

one acquired in 1944 became the Third No. 6]

The history of this little engine, or engines, is a bit of an enigma. According to Porter Locomotive Co. records, their engine with shop #1389 was sold in September 1892 to American River Land & Lumber Co. In the following November the Georgetown *Gazette*[13] tells of a "dinkey" hauled through town "to the track along Slab Creek." The engine made the trip divided between two large wagons so it may have had a tender like the one that shows in a picture taken after it was sold to the West Side Lumber Co.[14] It is no longer known whether this engine had a number, but in those early days Heisler No. 1 carried the number 2 on its boiler front number plate so this Porter was probably No. 1. It was sold to the West Side Lumber Co., then known as Hetch Hetchy & Yosemite Valley Railroad, around the turn of the century. The Heisler and the next four engines can be pretty well identified from newspaper stories as they arrived.

After Shay No. 5 came in 1903 another Porter 0-4-0T was bought and designated No. 6. Shay No. 7 came in 1904, so the approximate date of arrival for No. 6 can be fixed. For years No. 6 was believed to be the first Porter, brought to the South Side of the American River Gorge and finally given a number in the growing locomotive roster, but this view is probably wrong. A public auction notice in 1911, when the lumber company went on the block gave a Porter builder's number of #2049 to No. 6. Porter Co. records show shop #2049 sold to Issaquah Coal Co., Springfield, Illinois, in 1899. A check of cylinder stroke and bore suggest that #2049 has been with the company to date as No. 6 in the roster and is the one now on display in Camino along with Shay No. 2. How #2049 came to El Dorado Lumber Co. in 1903-04 is not known, though Issaquah Coal Co. had operations in the state of Washington and may have used her there. Porter No. 6 was to help old Shay No. 2 with switching around Camino. It was not often used, according to the memories of early engineers, and was virtually retired after 1915 when No. 11 arrived. In an early roundhouse fire it lost its fine wooden cab and got the less elegant sheet metal one it still wears. When put on display No. 6 was renumbered as No. 1 using the number plate from the Heisler, which helped to obscure the fact that Michigan-California Lumber Co. has had two Porter 0-4-0T locomotives.

No. 7

Shay 3C2T   Lima #868   Built 1904
Weight 66,000   Shipped 3/8/04
Cylinders 10 x 10   Drivers 28"
Boiler pressure 180   Tractive effort 14,800

Number 7 was bought for use between Camino and the summit of the 7% grade above South Cable. There it would take over the cars brought up by the Climax No. 4. The Climax would haul ten cars at a time to the summit from the cable. Number 7 would take 14-car trains into Camino and return. After the No. 10 came, the No. 7 was used only as a standby engine. Sometime in the 1930s it sported a homemade pilot snowplow, although snow is a minor problem on the South Side. Engine and plow were scrapped in 1951 when the narrow gauge was torn up.

It was hot in August of 1940 when the photographer visited Shay No. 7 at Camino. Naturally, the pilot snowplow was not to be seen. (*Russ Ahrnke Photo.*)

No. 8

Shay 3C2T   Lima #1628   Built 1906

Weight 100,000 (Dry 93,400)   Shipped 4/2/06

Cylinders 10 x 10   Drivers 32″

Boiler pressure 200   Tractive effort 22,580

Number 8 was the first big engine on the North Side. It was a wood burner as were all North Side engines until the late 1940s. (It is not known when the South Side engines became oil burners. They may have been converted as soon as they were acquired. One photo shows an oil transfer between standard gauge and narrow gauge in the early 1900s.) Number 8 was bought new, shipped either to Auburn or Folsom, and then hauled into Pino Grande by team, loaded on wagons. It was the last engine taken in that way. Starting with No. 9 they were disassembled and taken across on the cable. Number 8 was used to bring the logs into the mill from the woods replacing No. 5. The purchase of such a large, expensive locomotive suggests that the El Dorado Lumber Co., even after very large investments, was reasonably successful in 1906. A year later it closed down in the panic of 1907, not to reopen for four years. Number 8 remained the heaviest motive power on the North Side until No. 10 and then No. 6 (3rd) were taken across in 1943 and 1944. It was heavier than No. 6 (2nd), No. 9, No. 12 and No. 15, all of which arrived many years later. It was never converted to oil and in its last years was only used for switching around the camps. It was scrapped in 1950 along with all the other engines on the North Side.

Shay No. 8 arrived at Pino Grande all gleam and elegance. It was a massive load for a team to haul to Georgetown Divide, and remained the largest locomotive on the North Side for 42 years. It is pictured here before the Pino Grande enginehouse. In the background at the right is a Michigan wheel. (*R. L. Smirle Collection.*)

No. 9

Shay 3C2T   Lima #2662   Built 1913

Weight 84,000   Shipped 3/8/13

Cylinders 10 x 10   Drivers 29"

Boiler pressure 180   Tractive effort 17,000

This engine was built for C. D. Danaher Pine Co. which took over all the properties in 1911. It came knocked down and loaded on a flatcar, apparently in anticipation of the fact that it would be taken across on the cable. It was the first locomotive to reach Pino Grande in that way. Number 9 joined No. 8 hauling logs in from the camps. During the following thirty years the firm often had two camps using No. 8 in one and No. 9 in the other. After operations were extended beyond Camp 10, that camp became a division point or railroad camp with one engine, No. 8, to assemble trains there and another, No. 9, to take them from there in. Number 9 was converted to oil in 1946 and then was scrapped in 1950 with the other North Side engines.

The slab wood in the tender, below, is ample evidence that this picture was made before Shay No. 9 was converted to oil. At the right, Shay No. 10, on the first trip out in the morning with empty log cars, stops at the wooding up station just east of Pino Grande on the line to Camp 10. The man standing on the tender is Pete Boromini. *(Below: Pete Boromini Collection; Right: John P. Carrick Photo.)*

No. 10

Shay 3C2T   Lima #2756   Built 1914

Weight 100,000   Shipped 4/17/14

Cylinders 11 x 12   Drivers 32″

Boiler pressure 200   Tractive effort 22,580

Number 10 arrived from Lima at about the same time as No. 9. It was, however, fully assembled because it was to be used on the South Side. In size and detail, it was virtually identical with No. 8 which had been purchased eight years earlier. Number 10 went on the lumber haul from the cable to Camino and released both the Climax and No. 7 from the job. It could pull 12 loads to the summit where it assembled 24 loads for the trip to Camino. Three times No. 10 tipped over on trips to the cable. On one of these occasions it dropped a driveshaft which caught on a tie. It jill-poked over, the way a pole vaulter rides over his pole. Number 7 went over with it, but both were righted by the small, ancient Shay No. 2, using block and tackle. After the big three-truck Shays were purchased from Swayne Lumber Co. around 1940, No. 10 was converted to wood and moved via the cable to the North Side. It was probably welcome there, for the lumber company was logging in Camps 14 and 15, a long way from Pino Grande. Number 10 never went back to oil in the late 1940s when many other North Side engines were converted. It was scrapped with the others in 1950.

No. 11

0-4-0T   Vulcan #244   Built 1900 or 1901

Weight 30,000   Cylinders 10 x 14   Drivers 31″

Boiler pressure 150   Tractive effort 5,760

This engine was purchased in 1916 from the Folsom gravel pit, according to the recollections of one of the engineers still alive. Its first owners were Waddle & Fitch Co., Delaware, Indiana, and was their No. 7. After that it passed through the hands of P. W. Mc-Turk Coal Co. and then C. Cooper, who may have been a dealer in used locomotives, before C. D. Dan-aher bought it. Number 11 was used for switching around Camino whenever No. 2 was not available, which was not often. When the road was scrapped in the early 1950s, No. 11 was placed on display at Camino and is still there, along with Shay No. 2 and Porter No. 6.

For a saddle tanker, Vulcan No. 11 is rather impressive in bearing. Perhaps this is the reason it was placed on display, despite having given the company so little service. On the other page, Shay No. 12, very obviously out of service, was parked at Camp 10 during the late 1940s after it had been replaced by converted oil-burning engines. Apparently the headlight and other parts had been cannibalized. *(Below: Douglas Richter Photo; Opposite: John P. Carrick Photo.)*

No. 12

Shay 3C2T   Lima #2960   Built 1918

Weight 72,000   Shipped 1/16/18

Cylinders 10 x 10   Drivers 29″

Boiler pressure 180   Tractive effort 14,320

This engine was purchased in 1929 for $5500, including $250 worth of spare parts. It was used to haul logs into Camp 10 from Camp 11. Engines No. 8 and No. 9 then pulled them into Pino Grande. It had been No. 10 on the Iron Mountain Railway, owned by the Mountain Copper Co. of Keswick, California.[31] It was used on the North Side and presumably was taken across on the cable. Number 12 was cut up at Pino Grande in 1950 with all the others.

Second No. 6

Shay 3C2T   Lima #2924   Built 1911

Weight 72,000   Shipped 1/20/12

Cylinders 10 x 10   Drivers 29″

Boiler pressure 180   Tractive effort 13,000

The Second No. 6 was bought in the depression year of 1934 for $1350. It came from the Iron Mountain Railway, where it had likewise been No. 6. This was six years after the rebuilding of the cable and replacement of the little bobbie cars by Pacific Car & Foundry cars. The new cars had twice the capacity in green lumber and proved too big for Shay No. 5 so this new engine was put on the lumber run. Second No. 6 was used continuously on the lumber run from Pino Grande to Cable Point until 1942 when it went through trestle 28 while the latter was being repaired. The pieces of Second No. 6 were picked up but the engine was never put together again.

Second No. 3		
Shay 3C3T	Lima #3078	Built 1920
Weight 120,000	Shipped 2/5/20	
Cylinders 11 x 12	Drivers 32″	
Boiler pressure 200	Tractive effort 25,830	

The Second Shay No. 3 was the first three-truck locomotive on the narrow gauge track of Michigan-California Lumber Co. It was purchased in 1939 from Swayne Lumber Co. where it had been No. 2. The price was between $800 and $1200. The Second No. 3 took over on the South Side where No. 10 had been king since 1914, and alternated with Second No. 1, another Swayne engine, until the cable burned in 1949. It was cut up in 1951 with the rest of the South Side locomotives.

It was in June 1940 that the photographer caught the second Shay No. 6 for the picture on the opposite page, waiting patiently in the noonday sun on the track at North Cable while empty lumber cars were added, one at a time as they came across the cable, to the train which the 28-year-old Shay would soon be hauling around curves and over trestles to Pino Grande. The second Shay, No. 3, shown below, was a fine three-trucker for the company to use during its last 12 years of steam. The Shays built in later years showed many refinements not evident in the earlier models. This engine, for example, has a delicately flaring smokestack and a back-up headlight. Superintendent Smirle's casting on the crankshaft bearings is far more elegantly modeled than on the earlier Shays. The cab roof curves more gracefully. This was a lot of powerful machinery for $1200—even in 1939! *(Left: Al Phelps Photo; Below: Douglas Richter Photo.)*

Second No. 4

Shay 3C2T   Lima #2369   Built 1910
Weight 66,400   Shipped 9/16/10
Cylinders 10 x 10   Drivers 29″
Boiler pressure 180   Tractive effort 14,300

The Second No. 4 was acquired for about $680 in November, 1940, from Swayne Lumber Co. From 1910 to 1917 it had belonged to Truckee Lumber Co. as No. 3, and then to Butte & Plumas Railroad, a property of Swayne Lumber Co. Here it received its No. 4 designation. Michigan-California used it for switching around the camps until Second No. 6 went through the trestle in 1942, and then it was put on the lumber run from Pino Grande to Cable Point. Second No. 4 continued service there until the cable fire in 1949. It was the last North Side engine cut up in 1951, as it was used by the scrappers to remove North Side track. This was not unfamiliar work for the Second No. 4, as it had been used to scrap Swayne Lumber Co. trackage in 1940.

"No. 13" (?)
Plymouth Gasoline

Acquired in 1940, this was first used for switching around Camino. Later it worked a few years at the reload landing in Camp 15. It was at this landing that logs were shifted from trucks to railroad cars for the trip to Pino Grande. It was always called No. 13, but was probably never officially given that number.

Of these four engines purchased in the 1940s, the little Plymouth was a forerunner of days to come, when internal combustion would replace steam in the woods. (*Two upper photos: Douglas Richter; Two lower photos: John P. Carrick.*)

Second No. 1

Shay 3C3T   Lima #2926   Built 1917
Weight 120,000 (Dry 101,700)   Shipped 8/2/17
Cylinders 11 x 12   Drivers 32″
Boiler pressure 200   Tractive effort 25,830

The Second No. 1 was used with the Second No. 3 on the run from Camino to South Cable, and was almost a twin of its partner, except that it had piston valves instead of the usual slide valves. It was bought from Swayne Lumber Co. in January 1942. Swayne had bought it new in 1917, first numbering it 3, and later No. 1. It was cut up in 1951.

No. 14

Shay 3C2T   Lima #2183   Built 1909
Weight 51,200   Shipped 6/11/09
Cylinders 8 x 12   Drivers 28″
Boiler pressure 160   Tractive effort 9,490

track to a siding outside Camino and left there. The scrapping date is uncertain, but fans venturing to Camino after World War II reported that No. 14 was gone.

Number 14 was bought from M. J. Scanlon Lumber Co. in 1944, along with No. 15. There it had been No. 3. Still earlier it had been Marsh Lumber Co. No. 3, and then Feather River Lumber Co. No. 3. There is even some evidence that it belonged to Clio Lumber Co. before any of the others. Michigan-California had to take No. 14 in order to get No. 15 and paid $3200 for both. Number 14 had either once been standard gauge or was built by Lima for easy conversion. It was completely reconditioned in Camino, but was never used by Michigan-California, nor painted and lettered for them. It was towed down the

No. 15

Shay 3C2T   Lima #3212   Built 1923
Weight 93,700   Shipped 2/26/23
Cylinders 10 x 12   Drivers 29½″
Boiler pressure 200   Tractive effort 20,850

In May, 1944, Number 15 was bought from M. J. Scanlon Lumber Co. where it had been No. 2. It was taken across the cable and replaced both No. 10 and No. 8 on the long haul from Camp 15 to Pino Grande. Soon it was joined by the Third No. 6. It was an oil burner when purchased and was not converted to wood. Thus it was the first oil burner on the North Side. Later the Second No. 4 and No. 9 were converted to oil. This reduced the fire hazard, but more important was the fact that it took much less time to fill a tender with oil than it did to "wood up." Number 15 was cut up in 1950.

Third No. 6

Shay 3C3T   Lima #3306   Built 1927

Weight 135,500   Shipped 2/5/27

Cylinders 11 x 12   Drivers 32″

Boiler pressure 200   Tractive effort 25,830

This was the largest locomotive ever owned by Michigan-California Lumber Co. It had been built as No. 6 for Madera Sugar Pine Lumber Co. Feather River Lumber Co. bought it 11/6/35, keeping No. 6. When this firm folded in 1943, Hyman-Michaels Co. took it to San Francisco and put it up for sale. It was bought by Michigan-California in June, 1944, for $3075. Surprisingly enough, despite its size, it became a North Side engine and was taken across the cable. It was used on the long haul from Camp 15 in to Pino Grande and brought to an end the use of Camp 10 as a railroad division point. It was cut up in 1951 at Pino Grande.

Note: It appears that a locomotive was leased in 1912 by C. D. Danaher Pine Co. from the California Door Co. This latter firm operated the Diamond and Caldor Railroad another narrow gauge logging line in El Dorado County. This engine was, according to newspaper stories, destroyed in a Camino roundhouse fire in 1913 or 1914.

Shay No. 15 was parked at Camp 15, out near the end of the line, when the picture at the left was made in 1946. Standing in front of the counterweight house at the South Tower, the track auto has obviously seen better days, but probably it was never a thing of beauty. Michigan-California's "behemoth," the third Shay No. 6, is in action beside the pond at Pino Grande. *(Below: Al Phelps Photo; Left: Robert M. Hanft Photo; Left below: Douglas Richter Photo.)*

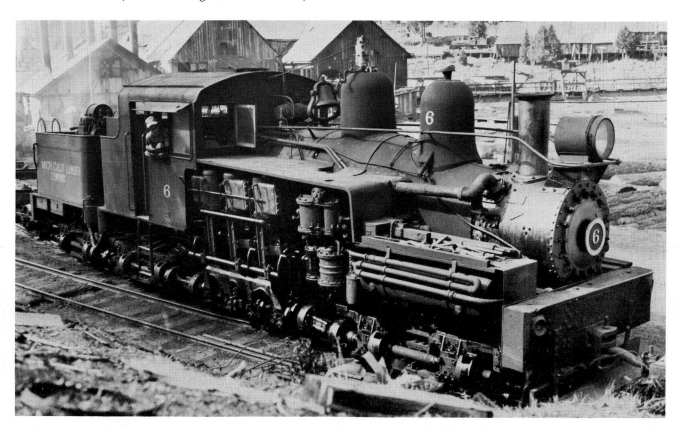

The Pacific Car & Foundry Co. lumber cars were longer and considerably more sophisticated than the old bobbie cars they superseded in the late 1920s, as will be evident on these pages. Brake wheels permitted application of brakes to both pairs of trucks at once. The picture above is best understood if one bears in mind the fact that the empty car is on the near track, with loaded cars on the track beyond it. *(Russ Ahrnke Photo.)*

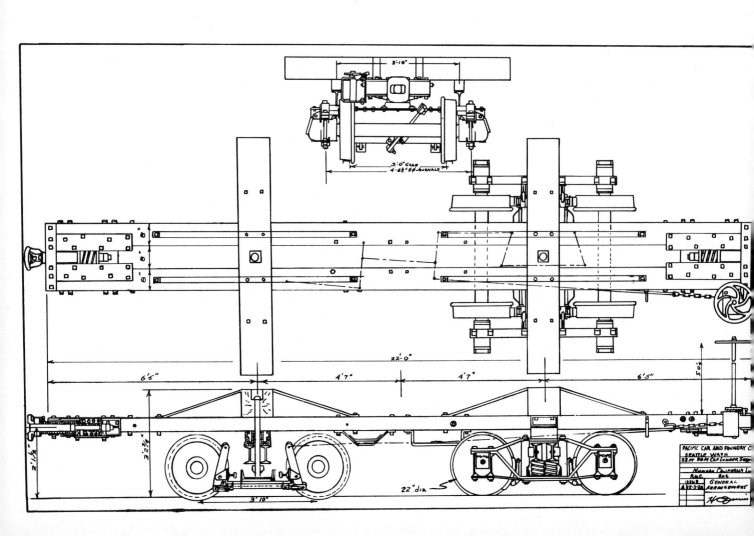

The old bobbie cars dated back to the turn of the century. Brakes were individually applied by poles fitted into sockets like the one seen in the photograph pointed toward the painted number. Even after the arrival of the Pacific Car & Foundry Co. cars, the bobbie trucks retained their usefulness in a variety of ways. *(Russ Ahrnke Photo.)*

MICHIGAN CALIFORNIA LUMBER CO.

TRANSFER TRUCK

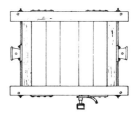

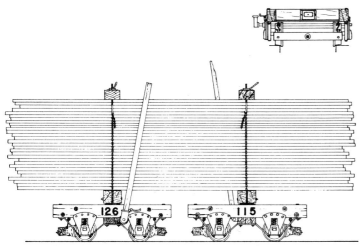

DOUBLE TRUCK LOAD USED AFTER 1902.

NOTES:

Color — Iron Work painted with dull red paint. Wood unpainted in later years, but may have been red when new.

Lettering — White, hand painted numbers.

Couplers — Link & Pin. Extra long links made from light weight rail. These cars used to haul cut lumber from the mill at Pino Grande to the finish mill at Camino. Single truck loading used with the first cable due to the weight limitation. The double truck loading system was used after the new cable was completed, however some loads were shipped by single truck on the second cable. Many of these cars later used as trucks on special cars for water, oil, fire wood, etc. No record of these cars being used as log buggies has been found.

TIMBER SIZES AND GENERAL DIMENSIONS

Main Sills	6" x 8" x 6'6"	Length Over Side Sills	6'6"
End Sills	6" x 8" x 3' 5 1/2"	Length Over End Sills	5'2"
Brake Beam	5" x 5" x 3'9"	Length Over Coupler Faces	6'5"
Center Cross Beam	4" x 12" x 4'6"	Width Over Sills	4'6"
Bunk	8" x 12" x 5'3"	Width Over Bunks	5'3"
Brake Lever	2" x 4" x 7 to 9'		
Wheel Dia.	14"		
Capacity: Single Truck	15,000 lb.	About 2500 Board Feet Of Lumber	
Double Truck	30,000 lb.	" 5000 " " "	

120023

Drawn From Photos By:
  Robert Brown
  Turrill & Miller Photo
  (The R. L. Smirle Collection)
  Russ Ahrnke
Additional Detail From:
  John Lewis
  R. Stephen Polkinghorn

VALLEY CAR WORKS

MICH-CAL TRANSFER TRUCK

Drawn 1-20-64 By *L.E.Klaus*

No. F-20   Sheet I of I

This water car demonstrates the ingenuity of company mechanics in improvising equipment from materials on hand. Here old transfer trucks and lightweight rail were teamed up with massive chunks of homegrown lumber to make this useful car. Obviously the car in the photograph, with only two braces on a side was not the same one as that depicted in the drawing, with five braces on a side. Evidently the crane on the opposite page was not improvised by local mechanics, at least in its original form. *(Russ Ahrnke Photos.)*

MICHIGAN CALIFORNIA LUMBER CO.

Water Car

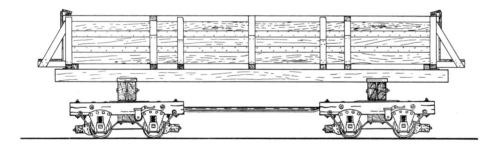

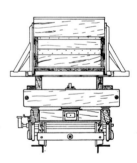

Section At Minor Braces

Section At Major Braces

Notes:

Trucks: The trucks for this car are rebuilt transfer trucks. Additional information on Valley Car Works drawing F-20. Photos show trucks to be older than the tank.

Timber Sizes: This drawing was developed from several old photos. Timber sizes scaled from photos and based on standard building practice.

Color: Unpainted sugar pine, several dark stains from seams.

Tank Liner: Light weight sheet metal.

This car was one of three similar cars.

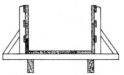

Drawn From Photos By:
Russ Ahrnke
Additional Detail From:
Robert Brown
R. Stephen Polkinghorn

121018

VALLEY CAR WORKS

MICH–CAL WATER CAR

Drawn 4-1-64 By *L. E. Klaus*

No. F-21   Sheet 1 of 1

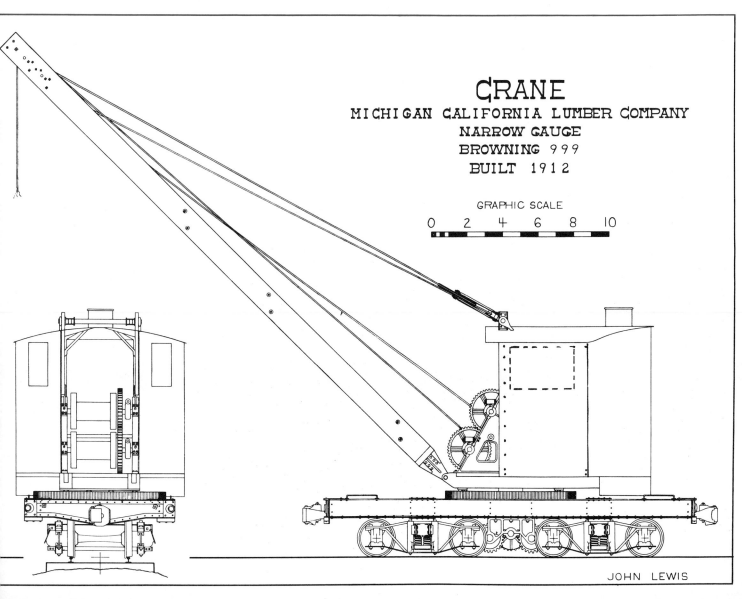

CRANE
MICHIGAN CALIFORNIA LUMBER COMPANY
NARROW GAUGE
BROWNING 999
BUILT 1912

GRAPHIC SCALE

0   2   4   6   8   10

JOHN LEWIS

Appendix C

LOCOMOTIVES AND EQUIPMENT OF
CAMINO, PLACERVILLE & LAKE TAHOE RAILROAD AND ITS PREDECESSORS

No. 1

Shay 3T   Lima #885   Built 1904
Weight 140,000   Cylinders 12 x 15   Drivers 36″
Boiler pressure 200   Tractive effort 30,000

This engine was specially built by Lima for the St. Louis Exposition of 1904. As soon as the fair closed, it went to the Placerville & Lake Tahoe where it was the only motive power until 1932. A woodburner until 1906, it was then converted to oil.

No. 2

Shay 3T   Lima #3172   Built 1922
Weight 140,000   Cylinders 12 x 15   Drivers 36″
Boiler pressure 200   Tractive effort 30,350

This engine was bought in 1932 from Hammond-Little River Lumber Co. of Bulwinkle, California, where it had been No. 4. Before that it had been No. 4 at Little River Redwood Co. It was donated to Traveltown in Griffith Park, Los Angeles, in 1955.

No. 101

Diesel   General Electric-Caterpillar   Built (?)
Weight 44 tons   380 horsepower

This $60,000 Diesel took over on the C.P.&L.T. in July, 1953, and is still in use.

Other Equipment

The road owned a homemade passenger car fitted up in 1905, but very little is known about it. Several cabooses have been owned, one at a time. Two of these show in pictures. The short one, which was also the last one, was wrecked in 1950, after which one was leased from the Southern Pacific. The Diesel locomotive was light enough so that no fireman was needed in the cab, unless a caboose was used. Thus, after the Diesel entered service, the lease with Southern Pacific was cancelled and no caboose was used again. The track and bridge crews had a flatcar and a couple of track autos with water tanks and pumps for fire protection.

In this 1938 picture, standard gauge Shay No. 1 retains the grace and distinction of its 1904 debut. The success of its basic design is evident in the strong similarity between it and its sister Shay, No. 2, built in 1922 with only superficial modifications— two air pumps, a backup headlight on the cab, cast trucks and the casting over the crankshaft bearings. The trim and unromantic successor of the two Shays appears opposite, next to Shay No. 2 in the Camino yard. *(Opposite: Michigan-California Lumber Co. Collection; This page: Douglas Richter Photos.)*

SOURCES

Superior numbers which appear in the text refer to the corresponding listings here.

1. *American Lumberman,* October 14, and December 16, 1905.
2. California State Board of Forestry, *Fourth Biennial Report.*
3. Drury, Aubrey. *The Livermore Family: Pioneers in California,* written in collaboration with Norman B. Livermore, Sr. Unpublished. 1953.
4. El Dorado *Republican.* August 15, 1901.
5. El Dorado *Republican.* November 7, 1901.
6. El Dorado *Republican.* November 12, 1903.
7. El Dorado *Republican.* December 17, 1903.
8. El Dorado *Republican.* March, 1904.
9. El Dorado *Republican.* March 9, 1917.
10. El Dorado *Republican.* January 25, 1918.
11. Folsom *Telegraph,* October 22, 1898.
12. Georgetown *Gazette,* July 23, 1891.
13. Georgetown *Gazette,* November 17, 1892.
14. Krieg, Allan. *Last of the 3-Foot Loggers* (Third Printing), published by the *Pacific Railway Journal,* Golden West Books, San Marino, California.
15. Unpublished manuscript, 1903, now in possession of Percy McNie.
16. Michigan-California Lumber Co., Company correspondence, June 26, 1930.
17. Michigan-California Lumber Co., Minutes, Board of Directors, November 17, 1917.
18. Michigan-California Lumber Co., Minutes, Board of Directors, February 25, 1918.
19. Michigan-California Lumber Co., Minutes, Board of Directors, December 1, 1922.
20. Michigan-California Lumber Co., Minutes, Board of Directors, April 13, 1946.
21. Michigan-California Lumber Co., Annual profit and loss statements for each year, 1918 to 1928.
22. Michigan-California Lumber Co., Plant Ledger, 1918.
23. Michigan-California Lumber Co., Plant Ledger, Camino Narrow Gauge Railroad Improvements.
24. *Pacific Coast Wood & Iron,* December, 1889, page 164.
25. *Pacific Coast Wood & Iron,* June, 1891, page 262.
26. *Pacific Coast Wood & Iron,* August, 1891.
27. *Pacific Coast Wood & Iron,* September, 1906, page 39.
28. *Pacific Coast Wood & Iron,* February, 1908, page 43.
29. Russell, T. O. *Slab Creek Survey Location Report,* 1926. There were apparently two Slab Creek surveys. Both are shown on the map. The one referred to here was on the west side of Slab Creek and was probably the preferred grade location.
30. *Timberman,* July, 1929.
31. *Western Railroader,* Volume 21, No. 2, page 13, December, 1957; also Volume 27, No. 1, page 13, January, 1964.

The original 1901 cable was powered by this steam engine with wooden teeth in its gear. The engine remained in place through two decades of operation by its electrically-driven successor until everything was torn out in 1949, after which this picture was made. *(Russ Ahrnke Photo.)*

Index